MORE MEMORIE
BRADFORD

TRUE NORTH BOOKS
DEAN CLOUGH
HALIFAX
HX3 5AX
TEL 01422 344344

THE PUBLISHERS WOULD LIKE TO THANK THE
FOLLOWING COMPANIES FOR SUPPORTING THE
PRODUCTION OF THIS BOOK

MAIN SPONSOR
SOVEREIGN HEALTH CARE

BENSON TURNER LIMITED

BRADFORD METROPOLITAN COUNCIL (MARKETS DEPARTMENT)

BRADFORD & BINGLEY BUILDING SOCIETY

THE BRADFORD PROPERTY TRUST LIMITED

R.S. CROOKE

A. DEWAVRIN LIMITED

ELTEX UK LIMITED

FILASPUN LIMITED

A.E. GOETZE AUTOMOTIVE LIMITED

GRATTAN PLC

HOLMES MANN & COMPANY LIMITED

KIRKGATE SHOPPING CENTRE

OILS & SOAPS LIMITED

ROSSEFIELD MOTOR COMPANY LIMITED

SCOTT (DUDLEY HILL) LIMITED

SYDNEY PACKETT & SONS LIMITED

STOBARTS (BRADFORD) LIMITED

P. WADDINGTON & COMPANY LIMITED

WHALEYS (BRADFORD) LIMITED

G. WHITAKER & COMPANY LIMITED

WHITAKER AND COMPANY (DENHOLME) LIMITED

THOMAS WRIGHT (BRADFORD) LIMITED

YORKSHIRE CO-OPERATIVES LIMITED

First published in Great Britain by True North Books
Dean Clough
Halifax HX3 5AX
1997

ISBN 1 900 463 16 4

Introduction

We were delighted with the reception received by the publication of *Memories of Bradford,* our last local book on the City. Many people took the trouble to write to us and we were heartened by the kind sentiments and helpful comments contained in their letters. All this encouragement has led us to bring out this latest offering, thoughtfully entitled *More Memories of Bradford.* Our aims have been similar to those which guided the production of our first Bradford book; entertainment takes priority over serious study, though the pages are liberally sprinkled with interesting facts, anecdotes and comment where appropriate.

Many local companies have allowed us to recount the history of their organisation on the following pages, and fascinating reading it makes too. Bradford has an impressive record where industry is concerned, not just in the area of textiles, for which it is obviously best known, but in a whole host of other business pursuits, many of which are described here. The Victorian men of vision who gave us some of our most beautiful buildings and created the wealth which enabled Bradford to grow and prosper get a well deserved mention in the book. We have not, however, forgotten the countless thousands of ordinary men and women with their own brand of gritty determination, who worked so hard in the mills and factories to make all this prosperity possible.

Great social changes have characterised Bradford since Victorian times which affected all aspects of local life. The main sponsor of this book, Sovereign Health Care, can trace its origins back to 1873 when the Bradford Hospital Fund was established. This was a time when all local hospitals were run as charities, and the success of the organisation grew to such an extent that by one year, in the 1930s, they provided 40% of the income needed to run the Infirmary. The story of the development of Sovereign Health Care, and the relevance it has to our lives in modern times is described at length. It makes intriguing and compelling reading.

There are some delightful pictures in the book of men and women at work in local places of employment, many of which will doubtless be familiar to readers today. Some of the companies from the past are recalled too, including Bradford's famous car manufacturer, Jowett, which later went on to build sturdy tractors at the Idle factory. Some excellent pictures from the time will revitalise fading memories and thoughts of friends and colleagues from times gone by.

The book covers a period between the 1930s and the late 1960s, the intention being to recall times within the lives of many of our readers. In common with most towns and cities, particularly in the north of England, Bradford has undergone many changes during this time. The impact of these changes on the lives of ordinary people seems easier to comprehend with the benefit of a decade or two's hindsight. The various developments were not always welcomed by the people they were supposed to help, but change was inevitable as a consequence of changing circumstances and a changing world. The growing level of car ownership, increasing prosperity and the demands of national retail chains were all catalysts which meant that wholesale changes to the architecture of Bradford were inevitable. Changes in the popularity of various forms of entertainment, particularly with the demise of cinemagoing in the late 1950s and 1960s would add to the impetus for change, as did the major reorganisation of the public transport system which included the demolition of Bradford's historic

The Alhambra and war memorial serve as reference points in this 1940s picture, enabling us to see the changes in this part of the city centre. The shops in the background were flattened in the redevelopment of the late 1960s.

railway station. When it came to shopping, Bradford led the way with innovative developments which were visited, and then copied by other local councils throughout the land.

The clearance of substantial areas of poor quality housing was a contentious issue in Bradford, as it was in most other thriving industrial areas. Everyone wanted to get rid of the damp, insanitary housing and communal outside toilets, but there was to be less enthusiasm for the high rise developments and sometimes impersonal estates which replaced them. Much of the development work which took place in the 1950s and 1970s was extensively photographed, and we have been fortunate to gain permission to reproduce the best ones in this book.

Bradford at play has been covered, with some delightful scenes from the ever-popular Lister Park Lido and boating lake at Wibsey Park. Shopping plays a part in all our lives and the importance of the activity is reflected in *More Memories of Bradford.* Kirkgate Market, the Swan Arcade, Busbys', Brown Muffs, and the growth of the Arndale development are all covered here, along with nostalgic scenes from virtually every busy shopping street you can remember. Sadly, for that is often an element in the nature of nostalgia, many of the buildings, shops and places we remember from our past are no longer with us. *Change* is taking place constantly in our city and, inevitably, our sense of perspective depends largely on our age and the experiences we have enjoyed... and endured. As we get older it is often easier to 'step back' and view the events which have shaped our lives in a clearer light. Of course, we are always pleased when readers write to us with their own memories of the places we feature so that we can add to the detail in future publications. When we began compiling *More Memories of Bradford* many months ago we expected it to be a pleasurable experience but our expectations have been surpassed. The quality of the photographs we have been privileged to use has been no less than superb - making the process of compiling the book a real joy.

It is our hope that the photographs and text contained in the following pages will rekindle a memory or two for you in an entertaining manner, bringing back to life the sights, sounds and atmosphere of times not so long ago. Whatever your age and interest in our great City, we hope you enjoy sharing this nostalgic backward glance. Happy Memories!

Mark Smith and Phil Holland
Publishers

TEXT
PHIL HOLLAND
BRIAN BURROWS
PAULINE BELL

DESIGN/DTP
MARK SMITH
MANDY WALKER

BUSINESS DEVELOPMENT
GARETH MARTIN

Contents

Right: The *Wright and Peel* rainwear shop, shown here in the mid 1950s, occupied a site in Town Hall Square that was formerly a billiard hall. The criss-cross pattern of the trolley bus wires, clearly visible in this picture, will bring back fond thoughts to many readers.

At your leisure

Left: This is a good picture of a traditional horse-drawn 'Piece Cart' operated by the Bradford Dyers Association. Its bow-top kept the driver dry as well as the pieces of cloth. They are now long gone and we wonder whether anyone had the foresight to preserve one? It is interesting to see the package being carried by the lady seen just to the rear of the Piece Cart. It is carefully made up with brown-paper and string, just as thousands of shop purchases

Top: This is the back of the St. George's Hall, built in 1853 and fronting Hall Ings, Bridge Street and Drake Street. Over the years the Hall has seen many uses; concerts, boxing, meetings and here as a cinema. It had been bought in 1926 by New Century Pictures who had used it prior to this. Part of the building was used as an hotel and sold Heys Gold Cup Ale. In the 1950s the hall was purchased by the Council and a new roof structure provided. It later reverted to its original use as a public hall. There is an organ in the property which has never been restored.

would have been in the days before paper, then plastic carrier bags.

The New Victoria Cinema became the Gaumont in 1950, around the time that the granite setts in Thornton Road would be covered with asphalt. The Broadcast Band and Becky Sharp receive billing outside the Theatre along the canopy at its entrance. The New Inn and the garage in its yard were swept away to make way for the construction of Prince's Way and the Police Headquarters.

Above: Broadway and The Ritz as they appeared in 1954. The view looks in the direction of Forster Square and towards Canal Road. On the left is the Swan Arcade with its billboards. The right-hand side has the Ritz Cinema which opened in 1939. It had become the ABC Ritz in 1950. The advertised film "Kiss Me Kate" was a '3D Ansco Colour Production.' Starkies outfitters occupied a curious, almost semi-circular ground floor premises with Mabel Ackroyd the florist next door. Blakeys had the shop unit to the left. Behind these shops was an entrance area for the Ritz which went through from Broadway to Leeds Road. The faience-clad building was eventually cased-in by the redevelopment in 1974 with one entrance left in Broadway when the building was made into a triple cinema. It is a sobering thought to consider that this scene was captured less than ten years after the end of the Second World War. Thoughts of sons and relatives who never returned from the war would still be fresh in people's minds.

"IN THE 1950s THERE WERE OVER THREE DOZEN CINEMAS IN BRADFORD & DISTRICT"

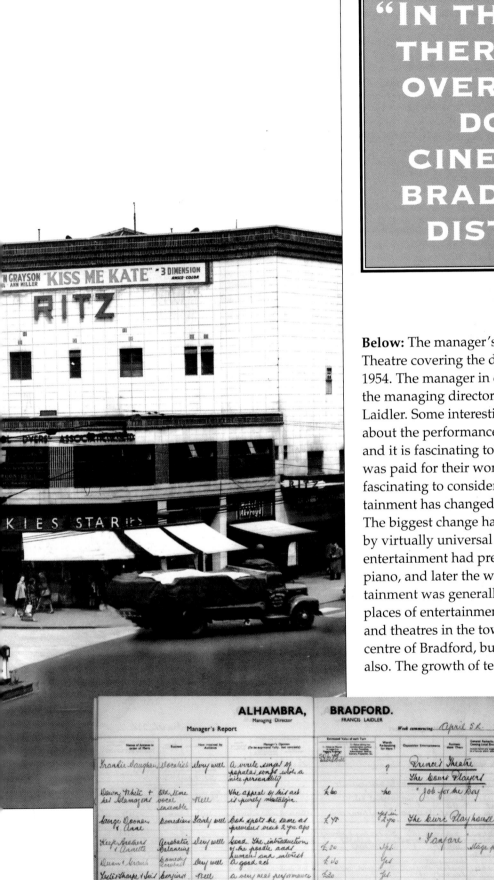

Below: The manager's report from the Alhambra Theatre covering the days between April 5 and 11th 1954. The manager in question was G. Barnes, and the managing director at the time was Francis Laidler. Some interesting comments were made about the performance of the artists' performances - and it is fascinating to see how much each of them was paid for their work. On reflection it is quite fascinating to consider how the world of entertainment has changed over the last fifty years or so. The biggest change has, without doubt, been caused by virtually universal television ownership. Home entertainment had previously revolved around the piano, and later the wireless set, and serious entertainment was generally only to be had in the many places of entertainment such as the many cinemas and theatres in the town. These were not just in the centre of Bradford, but dotted about the suburbs also. The growth of television ownership resulted in the decline of local cinemas, and most were to close or be converted into bingo halls by the 1960s. Times do change however, and it is remarkable how cinema-going has seen a resurgence in its popularity in recent years.

Right: Two or three girls can be seen studying this sign at Lister Park Lido. It reads 'DANGER keep off this cascade.' For over 40 years this was a popular venue for water-lovers throughout the district, helping to support the claim that Manningham's Lister Park was the most popular park in Bradford. The park itself had been opened in 1904 and the six-month exhibition organised to mark the opening was attended by the Prince and Princess of Wales.....not to mention two and a half million other visitors. It was the start of a tremendous run of success.

Left: Another scene from the Lido at Lister Park. The popular open air swimming pool was opened to the public in 1930. For most of its life the local facility enjoyed tremendous support from the residents of the city. Despite this support and affection of countless thousands of local people it closed in 1973 due to spending cutbacks. Later, in 1983, the Council decided that it could not justify the cost of serious repairs, estimated to amount to £60,000. Many a tear was shed in Bradford when the facility was finally demolished in 1991.

Above: Sun bathing and diving were equally popular when this scene was recorded at the Lido in Lister Park. Other water-related activities included boating on the lake as well as skating on the frozen water in winter. Nearby Cartwright Hall Museum was a popular haunt for Yorkshire people - particularly when it was either too wet or too cold to take a dip in the Lido. Bands were popular too, and crowds of people would attend them dressed in their Sunday best. When the end was in sight for the Lido in the late 1980s it became well-known for a more sinister reason. Drug addicts in particular found the secluded spot ideal for their sinister activities, and vandalism turned the once pristine public facility into an unpleasant, seedy magnet for the area's drop outs.

The boating Lake at Wibsey Park was the location for this photograph which dates from 1961. Messing about in boats was a popular pass-time on Bradford's park lakes. These days lack of interest and vandalism have combined to curtail this activity to a large extent. Most of us can remember days out on the water with dad or an elder brother... and the first time we were allowed to take charge of the oars ourselves to make unsteady, but enjoyable progress across the water.

Around the city centre

Manchester Road, as Christmas approaches just a few years after the end of the Second World War. The photograph is interesting for a variety of reasons, it cannot fail to evoke feelings of nostalgia in anyone who ever visited this area after dark, and the reflected light on the damp cobbles is guaranteed to bring back memories. The warm glow of the lights on the Odeon building would have attracted cinema-goers to the popular place of entertainment - at the time this picture was taken Anna Neagle and 'Sixty Glorious Years' were being advertised on the wall of the Oddfellows Arms, further along the street. The Majestic Bar 'one of Webster's Houses', can be seen on the right of the picture. You can almost hear the music from the badly-tuned piano drifting out of the smoky pub into the quiet street outside...

Below: A view showing the block between Market Street and Leeds Road (now Broadway) fronting Bridge Street, just before demolition in 1959, to make room for the Ivebridge House development. The building housing Barclays Bank can still be seen, it dates back to 1920. Ralph C Yablon the firm of solicitors is now part of the Kirkgate-based law firm of Temple Milnes and Carr. Demolition work had already commenced, note the open widows and evidence of removed balustrade from the top of the building. A sign in one of the former shop windows at the bottom of the picture gives notice of a 'compulsory removal sale.' This would become a common occurrence over the following years as the heart of Bradford was reshaped to meet the demands of the consumer age. Sadly, a by-product of all this improvement would be the loss of scores of small businesses which had served their customers well but were unable to afford the high cost of relocation to modern shop units.

Left: Looking along Bridge Street from Leeds Road to Tyrrel Street at the bottom of Sunbridge Road. The picture was taken in 1946. The Mechanic's Institute, which can be seen on the left, opened in 1873 and was demolished in 1973. Woods Music Shop can be seen in Sunbridge Road, they have now moved to Manningham Lane. Also visible is the

W.S..

Prudential Assurance Building, occupied by the District Bank, that substantial terracotta office block glowing bright red amongst a sea of stone and built in 1895. It still stands defiantly, but is now occupied by the Co-operative Bank rather than the 'Pru' Note how the ground floor of the antique china and glass shop is cut back for pedestrians, just like Victoria Chambers in Victoria Square. Walsh's Tobacconists occupied number 19 Bridge Street which has the large numerals '19' between the second floor premises. This block was demolished in 1959 to make the construction of Ivebridge House possible.

Above: This photograph gives a good view of Tyrrel Street as well as Market Street. An almost complete view of Town Hall Square and the "Crystal Palace." To the right we have the Keighley and Craven Building Society and the Yorkshire Penny Bank. Additional character is given to the scene by the Austin A40 on the right and the A35 on the left. The picture gives a lovely impression of what the centre of Bradford looked like on an ordinary working day in the 1950s. Much better than some of the 'posed' photographs that exist, this scene evokes real feelings of how we used to live around half a century ago.

Above: This photograph dates from shortly after 1950. This was the year that the New Victoria was renamed 'Gaumont.' The roundabout was blocked off to trams (previously they had been able to 'go through the middle') after 1949. The Alhambra had been painted maroon and white. Charlie Chester was top of the bill that week; do you remember "Down in the Jungle living in a tent... better than a 'Pre-Fab'... no rent !" From 'Stand Easy' on the wireless. The fine building, a source of pride for Bradfordians over many years, remains in place, though without the canopy that characterised it for so long. The War Memorial is still in place, as is the New Victoria Cinema, Ballroom and Restaurant, opened in 1930 and now known as the Odeon. James Stewart starred this week. Across New Victoria Street - now Prince's Way, we have Waltons Newsagents and Tobacconists, Halfords Confectionery and Battye's. Arthur Beckett, Grayston and Burrow, and Fred Truelove Turf Accountants occupied the offices above. The roundabout in Victoria Square awaits its stone walls and landscaping.

Above left: Tyrrel Street and Town Hall Square as they appeared in 1946. From left to right, we see the New Inns Magnet Ales sign along with Halfords Cycle and Motor Accessories shop. The white building is Collinsons Cafe. The tram is on No.2 route to Great Horton (White Horse) and would traverse the odd single track to the left of the double track. The Wibsey buses replaced the trams in 1945. Next is the Provincial Building Society block which has Burtons Tailors at the end.

On the extreme right the Guinness clock can be seen in Bridge Street. The lorry with 'PM' on the side is a coal wagon of Pearson and Moody fuel merchants. All the buildings mentioned are now demolished.

Left: Tyrrel Street as it appeared in 1946; the 'bobby' is on point-duty at the busy junction were Tyrrel Street met Thornton Road from the left as they both went towards Town Hall Square. Market Street goes off to the right. The tram tracks are still in use to Great Horton or Queensbury; they were to be closed in 1949. The Wibsey trams were withdrawn in 1945. On the left hand side of the street we have the Maypole Dairy Products shop (now defunct), a Thorntons toffee shop (the firm is still in business) Farmer Giles Milk Bar and that aromatic favourite, Collinsons coffee and grocery shop, with the restaurant famed for its 3-piece orchestra, and now all gone. The Empress public house which sold Hammond's Ales, brewed in Bradford, has been re-sited in Sunbridge Road. To the right of the street was the Provincial Building Society block with Burton's tailors at the end. The sign of the rubber shop can just be seen - it had a characteristic aroma very different from Collinsons coffee roaster. All this property was swept aside for the new provincial Building Society building, now known as the Abbey National.

Left: The imposing Town Hall clock tower, some 212 ft high, dominates this scene in a picture dating from 1952. The Tower and the end of the Town Hall can be seen along Market Street. The building was built in 1873, Lockwood and Mawson being the architects who beat off stiff competition to win the commission for the work. At one time there was an entrance to the right of the (right hand) telephone kiosk, the *frieze of kings* comes round from the front. A roundabout has been built in the Town Hall Square and the setts have been covered with asphalt. Street lighting is, by now of the fluorescent type. Notice too that zebra crossings have arrived - they superseded the old Belisha crossings but retained their orange Belisha beacons - now made to flash.

Above: This photograph from the early 1950s records daily life on Hustlergate, looking towards the Town Hall. The Swan Arcade is on the left with Colletts Gents outfitters; all to be demolished within the next ten years, along with over half the next block towards the Town Hall. On the right is the Wool Exchange, and on it can be seen the sign for the York County Savings Bank, now no longer with us.

Above right: This view shows the Town Hall from Market Street on a slushy day in the winter of 1940. The weather during this period became very severe. The Town Hall itself has the ground floor shielded by very large sand-bag buttresses which had been laid to protect the building from bomb blasts. No doubt every window would have been taped-up, or covered with blast netting to limit the amount of dangerous flying glass in the event of a German bomb attack. War had been declared in September 1939. The corner shop on the left appears to have been set up as a recruiting centre for the armed forces. On the left is a high-pressure gas lamp and a belisha beacon with an enamelled steel globe. Street lighting was reduced to zero at the beginning of the war with 'starlight' being introduced as the perceived threat of air-raids was reduced.

A grand building which served Bradford's textile traders for almost a century. The imposing style of the Wool Exchange was similar to the earlier Flemish cloth halls, and was known throughout the world to merchants and brokers concerned with the trade in wool and textile products. There are many really outstanding features incorporated in the original design, ranging from the high roof of the main hall and decorative beamed ceiling, to the beautiful marble pillars. The building had a lucky escape in the late 1960s when it was bought by the Council and tastefully converted for retail and office use.

W.S..

Daily life as seen along Market Street, looking towards Forster Square Station. This was 1946, before the railways were nationalised. It is dominated by the Wool Exchange which opened in 1867 with a clock tower 150 ft high. It is no longer an exchange, but carries out a useful function as a site for small shops and offices. As can be seen, small shops have always been a characteristic of this area, including the popular Spinks Bar.

W.S..

Left: The centre-piece of this lovely picture is a highly ornate street lamp and combined fuse-pillar, several of which graced the central area with Corporation coats of arms on the doors. This one appears to carry four arc lamps at the top and a pair of smaller filament lamps for use after midnight. The Ministry of Transport Act of 1919 resulted in main roads being given numbers and the pole shown here displays a very good set of road signs with the new road numbers. Other lighting along the street is by high-pressure gas lamps. This would have been a busy spot under normal circumstances; the newspaper seller has chosen it for this reason, and behind him a taxi cab awaits a fare with the same principle in mind.

The buildings on the left of the picture have been demolished as far back as the bank with the dome, this was the Bradford District Bank which was constructed 1873. Barclays Bank occupied one of the buildings which was to be demolished. The buildings on the right of the picture have also been demolished as far back as the Wool Exchange with the small spire. The umbrella shop has an umbrella outside it to act as an advertisement, as was often the practice at this time.

Right: An elevated view from Argus Chambers looking towards Bank Street (on the left) and Broad Street on the right. Broadway was one of the new Town Planning roads, 100ft wide, resulting from proposals made for Bradford's roads in 1928. The building in the picture bedecked with advertising hoardings is the much-lamented Swan Arcade (built in 1878) beloved of J.B Priestley and pulled down for Sam Chippendale's Arndale House. This heralded the age of 'concrete and car parks' which gripped the City in the 1950s and '60s. The adverts seen here are interesting and revealing: Eric S Myers 'No Worry' Depots sold Morris, Wolseley, Riley, Delage and Morgan cars. The Manningham Lane Depot was at Belle Vue.

The car park at the junction was probably run by the British Legion who specialised in this work. Eventually this area was built upon by Brown Muffs as Howard House, for their furniture and radio department. At the time of writing it is the location of the Yorkshire Building Society.

Some clues help us to determine the date when this photograph was taken: In the bottom left corner of the picture fencing around the site of the Bank Street Post Office can just be seen, so the scene was probably recorded before the Second War. There is a Belisha Crossing in view, complete with orange Belisha Beacons - named after Mr. Hore-Belisha, the Minister of Transport at the time of the 1930 Road Traffic Act.

Below: Danger! Men at Work...as demolition of the property fronting Leeds Road (now Broadway) round into Bridge Street and Market Street gets underway for the building of Telephone House and Ivebridge House in 1959. Passingham's Radio and T.V Shop had to move. Their slogan was '8 months to pay, no extra charge.' Adverts remaining are for 'Bush' and 'EKCO' brands. The Limbless Ex-Servicemen's Association also had to go. Cars parked include Morris Minor, Sunbeam Alpine, Austin A30 and A40, and Ford Anglia. 'KV' was, of course, a Bradford registration. The Provincial Building Society frontage to Market Street can be seen.

> "1947 SAW SERIOUS FLOODING IN BRADFORD CITY CENTRE - WITH A TORRENT DOWN THORNTON ROAD"

Above: Perplexed workmen look helpless as the force of water bursts an underground beck in the 1947 city centre floods. The pressure distorted the surface of the road to the extent that the wooden blocks which made up this section of the highway were dislodged and scattered all over the street. The location of this minor drama was Market Street and the Mechanic's Institute can be seen on the left of the picture.

Inset: 1947 saw serious flooding in Bradford, bringing misery to hundreds of shop-keepers and householders alike. In this photograph we see a torrent of water gushing down Thornton Road towards Tyrrel Street. The shop on the left of the picture is Halfords, the cycle accessories shop, and the notices above the main window advertises electric fittings and waterproof clothing. People on the other side of the street are seen taking advantage of the slightly raised situation of the area - using it almost as an island refuge in the flooded city centre which had caused so much disruption.

The floods would have added to the problems on the minds of ordinary folk in 1947. This was the year that the coal mines were nationalised and Britain was struggling to get back on her feet after the end of the War. On a brighter note, 1947 saw the marriage of HRH Princess Elizabeth and the Duke of Edinburgh, after a five month engagement. Lord Louis Mountbatten was enthroned as the last Viceroy of India in February 1947.

Below: The wide, modern thoroughfare we know as Broadway was a new road was actually constructed before the Second World War. At 80 feet wide it made a welcome contribution to the relief of Bradford's congested streets. This area changed beyond recognition in the late 1960s, as all the property except the buildings in the far distance, was pulled down. The delightful motorcars and overhead trolley wires in the photograph add to the nostalgic atmosphere it creates.

Lower down the street, on the left, hangs an interesting sign. It reads 'Gentlemen's Smoking Cafe.' An interesting concept for sure, but one which would not go down too well these days!

Below right: This model of the proposed redevelopments in the centre of Bradford dates from 1947. It was built to mark the centenary of the granting of Borough status to Bradford

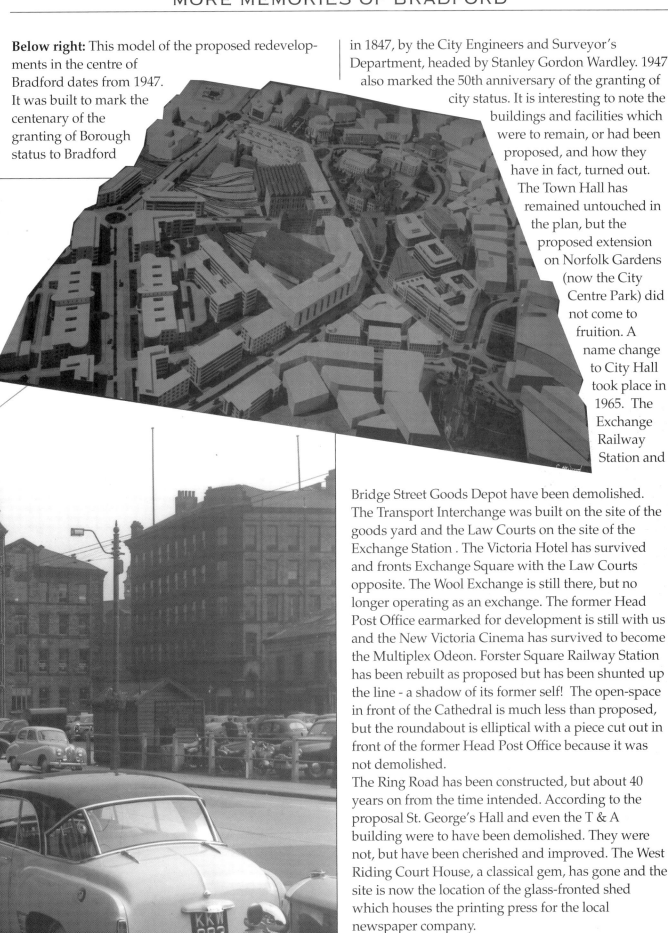

in 1847, by the City Engineers and Surveyor's Department, headed by Stanley Gordon Wardley. 1947 also marked the 50th anniversary of the granting of city status. It is interesting to note the buildings and facilities which were to remain, or had been proposed, and how they have in fact, turned out. The Town Hall has remained untouched in the plan, but the proposed extension on Norfolk Gardens (now the City Centre Park) did not come to fruition. A name change to City Hall took place in 1965. The Exchange Railway Station and Bridge Street Goods Depot have been demolished. The Transport Interchange was built on the site of the goods yard and the Law Courts on the site of the Exchange Station . The Victoria Hotel has survived and fronts Exchange Square with the Law Courts opposite. The Wool Exchange is still there, but no longer operating as an exchange. The former Head Post Office earmarked for development is still with us and the New Victoria Cinema has survived to become the Multiplex Odeon. Forster Square Railway Station has been rebuilt as proposed but has been shunted up the line - a shadow of its former self! The open-space in front of the Cathedral is much less than proposed, but the roundabout is elliptical with a piece cut out in front of the former Head Post Office because it was not demolished.

The Ring Road has been constructed, but about 40 years on from the time intended. According to the proposal St. George's Hall and even the T & A building were to have been demolished. They were not, but have been cherished and improved. The West Riding Court House, a classical gem, has gone and the site is now the location of the glass-fronted shed which houses the printing press for the local newspaper company.

The Alhambra did not go the way of so many similar establishments in other towns and cities, but is now refurbished and remains a great asset to the City. Arndale House replaced J.B Priestley's beloved Swan Arcade and the Odeon Cinema of 1947 has gone, to be replaced by the modern cinema mentioned earlier.

Above: It is impossible not to be impressed by the elaborate stonework shown in this picture of the Talbot Hotel. It was taken in the late 1950s and features the junction of Bank Street (on the right) and Kirkgate (on the left). The building which was the home of the Talbot Hotel remains in place to this day, though much of the area around it is now pedestrianised. The hotel was probably best known for the statue of the sturdy hound which looked down on prospective guests from the entrance porch. Sadly, the statues have now been removed. The busy corner retail unit was occupied by Hope Brothers the respected gent's outfitters. Lower down Bank Street the offices of the Halifax Building Society can be seen, and beyond them was the Wool Exchange.

Right: The elaborate and impressive premises of the Midland Bank at the junction of Darley Street and Kirkgate were erected by the Bradford Banking Company using Andrews and Delaunay as archi-

tects. The grand designs of turn-of-the century banks were, in part, intended to project an air of wealth and security to prospective investors, and this building certainly achieves that aim. At first, just one bay was built up Darley Street in 1858 and this was later extended to three. The building now houses offices of the Bradford and Bingley Building Society. Interestingly, Fowler and Oldfield are still engaged in the jewellery business.

Below: Well Street runs almost north westwards from the junction of Vicar Lane with Leeds Road. It was built in 1824 as a branch of the Turnpike Trust for Leeds Road - the new road to Thornbury and linked it to the old road - Church Bank at Forster Square. The trolley bus is on route 9 to Thornbury which commenced with trolleys in 1952 and ended as route 7 with the last trolley in 1972. The view is over the roof of The Junction public house which ended its days in a garish colour scheme. All the buildings in the picture which touch the junction have been demolished including the whole of the west side of Well Street. Petergate, the civic ring road from Forster Square joins Leeds Road at Eastbrooke Well around 50 or 60 yards behind the trolley bus. The scaffolded building undergoing demolition is where the Mechanics Institute was situated from 1840 until moving to Bridge Street in 1873 where it lasted for 100 years. It is now in Kirkgate, the street whre the first meetings were held in 1832. Bradford has more than its fair share of historic buildings and visitors to the City are frequently surprised at the quality and number of impressive works of architecture that abound in the area. Bradford architecture has, over the years, borrowed some of the best elements of design from all around the world; bell towers, temples and palaces to name but a few. The area is fortunate to be located on top of tremendous supplies of top quality stone. Indeed, quarrying has been a feature of local industry for longer than anyone can remember. Grattan Road saw stone quarrying as far back as Elizabethan times. A natural geological feature exists right under the city centre which takes the form of a layer of rock which is around 130ft thick. This has been put to use in the buildings and paving around our great City.

Above: A very nostalgic scene at the junction of Market Street and Kirkgate, just outside Forster Square where a point-duty policeman was essential to keep traffic flowing smoothly by 1956. Another officer was employed in the same role at the bottom of Cheapside, at its junction with Kirkgate. Lower Cheapside ran down the rear of the dark central block of property which was soon to be demolished for the extension of Cheapside itself. The new road formed a curve in front of Barclays Bank - whose buildings replaced that of the Bradford Old Bank to a re-aligned Forster Square. Properties, from the left, include: the Wool Exchange, built in 1867 and still, at the time, operating as an exchange; Barclays Bank (built in 1938-9) Spinks' Restaurant and the Boar's Head with Bodega Bar. The Bodega Bar (known as

the 'Bod' to regulars) was no doubt selling Hey's Gold Cup Ale, brewed at Wilson Square on Lumb Lane - sadly long since demolished. The building containing *W & J Williams (Removers)* offices has been pulled down too, (though the business carries on), and Lavells the tobacconists no longer operate from this location. On the extreme right is Commerce House; No. 24 Cheapside was formerly the home of Bradford Chamber of Commerce - the organisation later went on to work out of Pudsey! It was designed by Milnes and France for Beckett's Bank in 1885. At the time of writing this fine old structure is unoccupied. In the centre of the picture the large cast-iron box contains the electrical distribution fuse box, precariously located at the centre of the road, part of the transport system's direct current supply.

"BRADFORD TRAVELLERS MOURNED THE LOSS OF TROLLEY BUSES IN 1972"

Below: Forster Square from the Head Post Office, looking west. The YMCA building, formerly an hotel, was destroyed by fire in 1950. The layout of Forster Square had recently been remodelled and had a number of zebra crossings incorporated in the new scheme. These were a recent innovation. Broadway enters from the left, the street down the frontage of Forster Square Station is Kirkgate and this section in front of the curtain-wall was restored in 1997. It is now the Station Forecourt, resplendent with brick paving and a sculpture, 'Fibres' by the well-known artist Ian Randall.

Behind the station facade is the Midland Hotel of 1890, and, to the right, is Valley Goods Offices with a pretty dome. It still says 'Midland Railways' on the offices, though the company ceased to be known as such in 1923. Bradford travellers mourned the loss of trolley buses in 1972. Three of these vehicles can be seen in the picture.

W.S..

Above: Forster Square in 1952 had recently been remodelled and the carriageway asphalted - not a tram rail or granite sett in sight here! The stone-flagged footways are now concrete flagged. The last tram ran to Bradford Moor in 1949; the trolley bus ruled when this picture was taken and no loading was carried out from this centre island. The Head Post Office of 1897 sits in front of the Cathedral. This fine old building deserves a special mention here. It dates from the 15th Century and, like so many similar churches, has been rebuilt, modified and added to many times throughout its long history. The Cathedral was known simply as The Church of St. Peter until it became the Cathedral of the Bradford Diocese shortly after the end of the First World War. In a nine year period between 1954 and 1963 some of the most extensive modernisation took place, with low transepts being added and renovations to the East end of the building undertaken. There is some really outstanding stained glass in the church. The result is a Cathedral we can all be proud of, and a building which is well worth a visit.

Above: The changing face of Forster Square in the early 1960s is recorded for us in this photograph from the time. The picture shows how the roadway looked before the alterations were made to the main roundabout. Central House and the Boots block are completed, and give an indication of that style that would be adopted in the newly constructed shopping centre. On the left of the picture work was underway along Petergate, and the subways at Forster Square and Cheapside would be next on the list of projects to tackle. The network of poles and wires to deliver power to the trolley buses dominates the roadways in the picture and contrasts sharply with the modern construction work behind it. It is hardly surprising that the days of the trolley bus were numbered, particularly with the rise of more efficient diesel-powered vehicles and efforts to project an image of a modern new city.

Right: Modern architecture arrives in Bradford in the form of Ivebridge House, fronting Bridge Street, in a picture taken around 1960. This picture was taken soon after the building was completed. Denton's occupy the left-hand shop unit, now the Acropolis Coffee Bar, but the others were still to be let when this scene was captured. Britannia House, built in the 1930s, contrasts with the architecture of the 1950s. The Town Hall is to the right. A small triangular car park can be seen at the centre-bottom of the picture. It is attended by a British Legion Member and, interestingly, it is covered by wooden blocks which formerly covered Market Street until they were lifted by flood-water. Bradford really was at the cutting edge of town centre development in the late 1950s and '60s. The drive to create modern new shopping centres and accommodate the growing needs of the motorcar pre-occupied officialdom for over 30 years.

Below: A familiar face in an unfamiliar role. Fred Trueman did much for Yorkshire cricket and the Arndale Centre did much for the world of shopping. Both have seen their fair share of controversy over the years too. This scene was recorded at Sam Chippendale's ground-breaking monument to retailing, where the famous cricketer is performing the traditional 'topping-out' ceremony. The building is located on the site of Bradford's beloved Swan Arcade which was pulled down in order to drag Bradford into the brave new world of modern shopping. Other cities were destined to follow Bradford's example.

Sovereign Health Care - 125 years of caring for the people of Bradford

In Bradford, in 1873, the Bradford and District Hospital Fund was founded, with the purpose of raising funds for local hospitals. At that time all hospitals were run as charities and it speaks volumes for the keenness of the Bradford members

When the National Health Service was set up in 1948 and the British public generally no longer had to worry about the expense arising from illness, only 32 hospital funds remained in existence and the rest were wound up. The Bradford Fund was

that, in one year in the 1930s, they provided approximately 40% of the income needed to run the Infirmary.

In 1933 they had their reward when the New Contribution Scheme allowed members to have free treatment from certain hospitals and convalescent homes in return for their regular weekly contributions. Five years later, the scheme expanded its business beyond Bradford and District by becoming a founder member of the British Hospitals Contributory Schemes Association.

one of the 32, and in line with their customer's changing needs began with the provision of cash benefits, helping members meet the cost of everyday health care. Aneurin Bevan said of them, and those like them, "People of such experience will find new fields to cultivate if they watch where the NHS shoe pinches." Bradford members renewed their voluntary efforts to help ease the pinch and provide themselves with additional peace of mind.

The Bradford and District Hospital Fund's December newsletter for 1958 reported that the Charities Fund for that year had provided £1,000 for alterations and repairs to Craig Convalescent Home for Children at Morecambe, £156 for furnishing a day room for elderly patients at St. Luke's Hospital, Bradford and £850 for a sports pavilion for patients and staff at Westwood Hospital, amongst numerous other donations.

Over the years, frequent gifts were made to the Yorkshire Cancer Campaign, the Bradford Women's Home

and the Bradford Cripples' Association. In the 1960s the Fund assisted Bradford Association for the Physically Disabled with its new building fund, provided geriatric chairs for Thornton View Hospital and helped to extend the hostel run by the Bradford Association for Mental Health.

In 1965, Sovereign's main challenge was to develop the Shilling Scheme which was temporarily hampered by the destruction of the Fund's offices by fire. In December 1968 the Fund assured its members that 'The income of the Charities' Fund consists entirely of the dividends and interest on the Fund's investment and no allocation whatsoever is made to it from the Contributory Scheme.'

1973 was the Bradford Fund's centenary year. The then Chairman, Mr. C.P. Dawson reported that the benefits paid out during the year were to a value of £300,000 and that receipts amounted to £400,000. *Continued overleaf*

Above: A view of Manningham Lane dating from the 1920s. Left: The Theatre Royal, site of the new Sovereign Health Care premises, Royal Standard House on Manningham Lane. Centre, left: Another fund raising event in 1934. Facing page, top: Another picture of the Theatre Royal, dating from the very early part of this decade. Facing page, bottom left: An illustration of the company's old Vicar Lane premises, dating from 1976. Facing page, bottom right: Herbert Gill, Chairman of the Bradford Hospital Fund from 1914 to 1936.

From previous page
He thanked volunteer management, paid staff and investors. The Centenary was celebrated by a dinner at the Norfolk Gardens Hotel in October of the same year.

In 1974, the Shilling Scheme (by now the 5p Scheme) was closed and replaced by the Super Scheme. This went smoothly with most members choosing to transfer. Sadly, by the 70s, the organisation's newsletter had ceased to report in detail the charitable assistance given but at least we know that in 1974 two vehicles specially adapted for carrying patients in wheelchairs were presented to the local social services.

1976 brought the Sovereign Plan, the main aim of which was to enable members to make provision in the event of serious illness to receive benefit at a rate appropriate to their needs. The scheme led to an increase both in unit contributions and in numbers of new members. The Chairman urged members to consider taking three units at a cost of

30p a week "a very reasonable figure....less than the price of 20 cigarettes"! Employers were urged to provide health care for their employees with Sovereign's help.

By 1976, the newsletter had been enlarged. Details of charitable donations were available again and members' letters invited and published, in the main giving thanks for benefit payments made. "Did you know," the '76 edition stated, "that of the new members joining the Hospital Fund, 58% are men and 42% are women?"

In 1977 the minimum contribution became 20p and the Fund's target of 50,000 units was reached. For the first time, benefit paid out in a year exceeded one million pounds. A His 'n' Hers option was introduced with the slogan 'The easy way to join and Pay.' It dealt with the problem of members who wished to contribute through their

employment on behalf of their partners who weren't employees.

Into the eighties and the leader article of the Fund's members' newsletter is urging "the 30p per week figure which really should be the sensible contribution if members are to ensure that their entitlements cover their needs." Charities to benefit from the Fund in '81 included the Bradford and Airedale Whole Body Scanner Appeal, the British Epilepsy Association, the Bradford Day Shelter and Baildon Venture Scouts. In 1982 the cost of a unit changed from 10p to 15p in an attempt to ensure that benefits kept pace with inflation. It was thus possible to make the new minimum Hospital benefit £56 a week and improve maximum entitlements on other benefits. September '82 saw the first of many thousands of records being input to the new ICL system 25 Computer.

Under the new title, Sovereign Health Care, which became the registered trading name in 1986, the organisation has grown to a membership of over 134,000 nationwide. It remains a non profit-making organisation which exists entirely to help its members meet the cost of caring for their health. The wide range of benefits which Sovereign Health Care provides has developed over the years, in line with the cost of health care items such as dental treatment, optical care, chiropody, physiotherapy and acupuncture.

The main benefit offered is still cash for the event of a stay in hospital, which means that in such a vulnerable position members still have peace of mind. Today's plan is offered for both individuals and company employee members who can choose to pay any of the seven contribution levels ranging from £1.00 to £4.00 a week.

Sovereign Health Care is a member of the British Health Care Association, about which another politician, Stephen Dorrell in 1991 said, "It seems to me that BHCA member associations are a perfect example of this country's national genius for the ability of our institutions to evolve to changing needs....I welcome the continuation of the work done by BHCA member associations and the social support that they give the National Health Service."

The BHCA had come into being after the 32 persevering Hospital Funds, which had banded together to become the Association of Contributory Schemes in 1931 continued to lobby their important role within the non profit-making health care arena. The BHCA is anxious that the Fund's work shouldn't be confused with private medical insurance and has pledged its continuing support for the NHS. So far charitable contributions to NHS hospitals have been more than £15,000,000.

continued overleaf

Above: Fundraising events have always been a major part of Sovereign's business. This mini-bus was bought with proceeds from various charity events hosted by the company and presented to the Bradford Social Services in the early 1970s. **Above left:** *Much needed equipment for a local hospital, purchased by Bradford Hospital Fund and presented to the director of the hospital by Mr Eric Bentham, chairman of the BHF at the time.* **Facing page, bottom:** *An artist's impression of what the new building on Manningham Lane looks like.* **Facing page, top:** *A happy picture of the baby weighing competition at a Low Moor Carnival in 1939.*

From previous page

They also organise, annually, a national campaign to recognise and reward the efforts of people working in or alongside the NHS. As a result of their British Health Care Awards, dozens of doctors, nurses and carers, nominated by the general public receive the Fund's financial support.

Sovereign Health Care also offer an Accident Plan. In addition to its individual contributors, Sovereign now has in excess of 1,750 corporate customers which include large blue-chip companies, the public sector, unions and the civil service.

Above: Sovereign's Chief Executive, David Lewis presenting a Nurses Training Grant to a BRI nurse to help advance her studies. Left: A Massive £1 million fund raising project currently undertaken by Sovereign Health Care and Bradford Hospitals NHS Trust. Below: Sovereign's generous support helps the Bradford Friends of the Foundation for the Study of Infant Death to purchase ten baby care monitors for St. Luke's in Bradford.

Sovereign continues to be commended for its Charities Fund which works alongside thousands of registered health and hospital related charities throughout the UK.

Sovereign Health Care can be contacted on Bradford 729472.

Health care is about the everyday quality of life. "How are you keeping?" is a common enough question and most of the time the reply is "Fine." It is when the answer is different that Sovereign Health care comes in.

At work

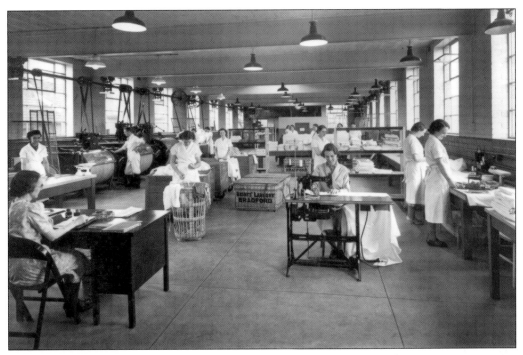

the lady in the foreground; perhaps she was the supervisor tasked with running a tight ship in the department, or the person in charge of the accounts?

Below: Skilled workers engaged in the production of fur coats and mink stoles in the *Fur Workroom* of Busbys' Store. The department could boast very little elbow-room, situated as it was

Above: A very neat, well laid out, clean and tidy scene recorded at Busbys' laundry department. Here we see the men and women involved with the service which included washing, ironing and mending. Of course, Busbys' store generated plenty of laundry work in its own right - from the cafeteria to the staff uniforms and towels. On top of this the service was offered to customers and other businesses, all designed to keep the staff in this picture busy and the tills ringing. This scene clearly shows the overhead *lineshaft* which carried power to the various machines used in this department. It was typical of many before small electric motors became readily available. The staff look happy enough, though the work must have been rather repetitive. We can only guess at the role of

at the top of the store between the gables. A variety of animal skins can be seen being worked upon here. At least one of the men in the photograph is wearing a winged-collar; the type of clothing worn to work was even more of an indication of the rank and impor-tance of the position held by an employee than it is today. The work looks very labour intensive. Notice how all the supervisors in the picture are men - entirely typical of the era. Fur coats were something of a status symbol among women for many years, often the special gift for an important anniversary or occasion. If an entire coat could not be afforded then a fur stole was the next best thing. There was a ready market for fur products... and Busbys' was ready and equipped to serve it.

Right: How we used to be. Home time seen from one of the gates at Salts Mills, the largest employer in Shipley until it closed. Workers knew this location as the 'Penny Oile' near the railway bridge. At least one interesting item of clothing can be seen in the picture. The army battle-dress jacket worn by at least five of the men coming out of the mill. A reminder of National Service or wartime action, no doubt. The photograph probably dates from the late 1950s, when National Service, the compulsory two years in the Forces for every healthy male over eighteen years of age, was coming to an end.

Below: Bradford was built on the textile trade. Textiles provided employment for thousands of men and women over the years as well as the wealth from which the town's best known civic buildings public facilities and parks were constructed. Trade multiplied after the first steam engine was employed in the production process, and Bradford assumed a worldwide importance in everything related to cloth. Bradford's first steam powered spinning mill was introduced in the year 1800 on a site near the centre of the city. The production of all types of textile fabric was followed, quite logically, by rafts of industries designed to turn the finished cloth into curtains, furnishings, uniforms, suits, coats, dresses and every other kind of fabric imaginable.

Left:: This picture will bring back memories to anyone who worked in a textile mill, and goodness knows how many thousands of our readers this will apply to. The experience of working in a textile environment was like few other jobs for it was demanding in so many ways; memories are of the noise which was relentless during working hours and prevented all but the most basic communication.... until lip-reading had been mastered; the characteristic smell, depending on the particular job being performed and fabric being worked, would permeate the workers clothes, to the extent where it would fill the whole of the buses and trams taking them to and from the mill; and, consider too, the strain of standing up all day performing repetitive tasks, in hot weather and cold, often for 20, 30 or 40 years with only minor changes in the working routine.... life really was hard for the workers in Bradford's textile mills.

Above: A scene from the interior of a Bradford textile concern which is typical of similar factories operating from the mid-1950s onwards. This is clearly not an ancient picture; note the fluorescent lighting, corrugated metal roof and steel ducting for the heating and ventilation. The working area is neat and tidy and the five people in the scene are busy with their Jacquard weaving looms. Textiles, as an industry has had its ups and downs over the years, but Bradford has played a leading role in the activity for over 500 years.

Above: A typical scene in a typical Bradford textile mill works canteen. This truly delightful photograph shows a workforce made up mainly of young women, though there are one or two men present in the background, enjoying their lunch break in the middle of a busy day. We would love to hear from anyone pictured here so that we could add to the detail contained in future reprints of this book. The photographer has done well to capture the really natural facial expressions of the young ladies seated nearest the camera. They were obviously too hungry to stop eating for more than a moment. And look at that food. No healthy eating menus here, just good old fashioned stodge to warm you up and get you ready for the hard work of the afternoon. Still, it doesn't appear to have done these girls any harm - despite their simple working clothes they all look as pretty as a picture as they enjoy their well-earned break.

What topics would the conversation cover as the young ladies relax, away from the terrible din in the weaving sheds? Of young men for sure, and of trips to the *pictures* and dancing at Bob Gledhill's at the weekend.... or perhaps hours spent beside the juke box in Farmer Giles Coffee Bar on Tyrrel Street? Near the Alhambra's stage door the Olympus coffee bar would have been a regular haunt for youngsters too.

Below: This thought-provoking photograph gives an impression of what working life was like for around 100 ladies employed in a 'burling and mending' department of a large local textile concern. Viewed against the scale of Bradford's involvement in the textile industry, this post-Second World War scene is relatively recent. Many books exist which chart the progress of Bradford's historic share of textile activities from the early days in the 13th century when it began to grow, through the hand-loom days to mill-based production which saw the town play a leading role on the world textile stage. This century has seen some notable fluctuations in Bradford's success in the industry, all considered important in view of her historic reliance on textiles for the vast majority of local jobs and subsequent civic prosperity.

At the dawn of the twentieth century Bradford could look back on 100 years of unprecedented growth and a transition from a landscape of squalid over-crowded houses with poor public services, to a growing town with fine architecture and continually improving housing conditions. Work was generally not difficult to come by and all manner of public services, including places of entertainment, transport and public parks were developing in the area.

The outbreak of the Second World War underlined Bradford's national importance as a textile producer, and the mills received welcome new business in the form of government orders for uniforms, tents and blankets. Up to three-quarters of mill output during the period was related to government war contracts.

The Depression spelled the end for many textile mills and textile unemployment blighted Bradford in the early 1930s. Failure to invest in modern methods, along with cheap foreign imports, led to a decline in the local textile industry as the century progressed. Recent times have seen the demolition of many mills and the conversion of others, such as Shipley's Salt's Mill into business parks, arts centres and retail centres.

Top: Bradford's Wool Exchange was opened in 1867. The foundation stone had been laid by Lord Palmerston, the Prime Minister of the day. As was the tradition during this period, a competition had been run to decide which firm of architects would be commissioned to design the building. It was won by Lockwood and Mawson. Henry Francis Lockwood also designed Salt's Mill and Titus Salt's statue which is now located in Lister Park. The Wool Exchange once performed a role central to the trade in wool in the district and beyond. At one time there were 2,500 members who operated in every market in the world. Buyers and sellers would meet on the floor of the Wool Exchange for trade in every type of wool or hair, from locations spread over the four corners of the earth. The fine building where this trade was once conducted was bought by the Council in 1968. It was recently refurbished at a cost of £2.5 million and now houses a leading bookshop and other shops and offices. The Hustlergate side of the building was renewed with a controversial glass fascia to complement its Revived Venetian Gothic Style which incorporates the pink marble pillars which can be seen in this striking photograph.

Right: Lister and company operated Manningham Mills on Heaton Road and Lilycroft Road. It was one of the largest concerns of its type in Bradford. Velvet was their speciality and here we see the packing department for the despatch of Lister's 'High Pile Velvet' to all parts of the world.

Below: Fearless Steeplejacks and their ladders can be seen high upon 'Listers Pride' - the ornate chimney of Manningham Mills - once the largest silk mill in the world, with 16 acres of floor space. The chimney is 250 ft high and 11 ft square internally at the top. Measuring the photograph itself suggests that the flat top has a width of 4 feet; too narrow to 'drive a carriage around' as reputed. Nevertheless, this 8,000 ton Italianate leviathan is very impressive. The mill has a frontage of 350 yards to Heaton Road and 150 yards to Lilycroft Road. It has two, six storey blocks as well as the lesser buildings. The mill dam was situated across Lilycroft Road, the site is now occupied by Lawfield House - the local Toller Lane Police Station.

Oiling the wheels of the textile industry

John Hellewell & Sons Ltd. was set up in 1874. From its premises in Walker Terrace off Wakefield Road, the business dealt primarily in oils used for lubrication and processing in the textile industry. Its fortunes, dependent on textiles, rose and fell according to the health of its customers with a dip during the war years when rationing of raw materials slowed the production of fabrics.

The textile trade declined throughout the 1950s so that stern measures were required. In 1963, tired of 'going it alone', Hellewells amalgamated with two other companies. One of them, Gledhills of Scoresby Street in the centre of Bradford, was in the same line of business and it was their premises that became the base for the new group, Oils & Soaps Ltd.

The other new partners, Salmon and Nephew, were soap merchants. The Company turned tallow (fats from animals) into soaps and auxiliary products, also required by the textile trade. They were a thriving concern, operating from a factory in Valley Road, but their neighbours found the tallow smell offensive and environmental regulations obliged them to close it down.

Fortunately, Salmons' managing director was a good friend of his opposite number at John Collier, who agreed to make soap for him. Colliers are still in business today.

By the 1970s the textile industry no longer required their products and Oils & Soaps switched to making detergent-based cleaning materials. The Company obtained contracts for detergents to clean all the Bradford schools and for supplying the '5-Minute Car Wash' company's branches throughout the country. The raw materials were bought in and mixed and blended at the factory which has grown to keep pace with the rapidly expanding chemical industry.

Now their customers are mainly institutions such as commercial and hospital laundries, the concrete industry and contract manufacturing. They produce a standard range of laundry products, cleaning chemicals and concrete mixtures as well as new and advanced products. By 1971, the construction of the Bradford Inner Ring Road had finally been decided upon. Oils and Soaps, perhaps hoping that their prompt co-operation would be rewarded by council generosity, were the first company to move out of the Scoresby Street premises, pre-empting compulsory purchase. They purchased and moved into their present premises.

The original partnership of Oils & Soaps Ltd did not last very long before David Hellewell bought out his partners and became managing director. His son Peter succeeded him so that the firm was run by its founding family until Mr F Braithwaite, the present MD took over. The Company was sold in 1997 and is now part of Wilton Investments Ltd.

continuously investigating new raw materials and processes for all areas of the business.

Above: The impressive premises of Oils & Soaps Limited on Rutland Street. Facing page, top left: John Hellewell, founder of the Company who died in 1913. Facing page, bottom right: David Hellewell on the left in the 1940s. With him is Dennis Swaine, the only other employee at that time. The picture was taken at the original premises on Wakefield Road. Left: The Company has a thriving and ever increasing blending operation for both powder and liquid products. Below: The warehousing facility at Eastwood Street, pictured here with the modern fleet.

The Rutland Street site contains administration and manufacturing whilst the distribution of finished goods is dealt with from the warehouse at Eastwood Street. The Company maintains a well-equipped laboratory with a technical team which provides quality control, ensuring all raw materials, processes and finished goods conform to the exacting requirements of ISO 9002. Their technical service provides support for field staff and problem-solving for customers. There is a dedicated development team

Whitaker & Co (Denholme)Ltd - Craftsmen in wood for almost a century

Today, to the Bradford man-in-the-street, this company name is synonymous with high performance windows and timber staircases. These are produced for both domestic and commercial premises and offer 'tailor-made' solutions to builders' problems whilst using volume production methods.

All this is a far cry from the Whitaker and Company founded by Esau Whitaker in 1900. At the Old School,

at Edge End, he set up business as a joiner and undertaker. In those days, the best available power for the machines was provided by a temperamental gas engine.

Esau's three sons joined the business in turn, Harry, the eldest leaving school at 14 in 1916, Jack in the 1920s and Fred, after attending Keighley Grammar School, in 1930. Fred took charge of administration and buying, leaving Harry controlling manufacturing whilst Jack looked after sales.

During the early 1930s more electric power was needed to serve the increased mechanisation. The Electricity Board could only supply the outskirts of the village with such requirements and so land at Denholme Gate was purchased from the local mill owner, Garnett Foster and a new factory was built in 1933. All four walls of this original structure have now been pulled down for subsequent extensions, but the factory was the foundation for the present complex. Soon afterwards, when an adjacent farm went up for sale, Whitakers' offered one thousand pounds for one of the fields adjoining the factory. The farmer was asking only twice that amount for his

whole property and so the company bought the lot.

The Second World War brought changes as many of the workforce, including Fred, were drafted. The firm's premises were taken over by the Admiralty. They used the buildings for storage, whilst the company moved its manufacturing operations back to the Old School, which had fortunately been retained. Whitakers' valuable contribution to the war effort was to make ammunition boxes, life rafts and army barracks.

At about this time, after only a short retirement, Esau died and, fittingly, the company made his their last coffin.

The age of specialisation was beginning and so the firm rationalised its products so that today, only windows, external door frames and stairs are made.

After the war, the plant moved back to Denholme Gate and the firm played its part in the nation's massive re-housing programme. In 1952 it became a limited company with a well established and respected name within the joinery industry. The present office block and some extra factory accommodation was built and yet further expansion followed.

By now, the family had grown. Fred remained a lifelong bachelor but the firm had been joined by Jack's two sons, Rex and John, and Harry's son Keith. Sadly, John died in 1963, aged only twenty three after working less than four years. Soon afterwards, Esau's sons died in quick succession, Fred whilst still in service in 1969 and Harry and Jack after short retirements.

Rex and Keith Whitaker managed the company jointly from then until Rex's death in 1983. His widow, Joyce then joined the company as chairman with Keith as managing director. The company prospered through to the late 1980s and despite the severe recession of the early 1990s, improved their quality to such an extent that they achieved the coveted BS5750 (BS EN 9002).

Keith's daughter, Carol, joined the company in 1982, followed by her sister, Joy, in 1990, thus continuing the family tradition into the fourth generation.

The firm has found time to take an interest in the wider community. The family has always been supportive of the Denholme branch of the Royal British Legion and the British Woodworking Federation. They have also supported the local Anglican church, both financially in the repair of its spire and practically in the manufacture and fitting of an internal screen.

Whitakers have demonstrated their technical superiority by helping to pioneer new techniques in timber

conversion and drying, a process known as 'green-split'. Also, they are currently involved with Imperial College, London, and Akzo Nobel on a new preservation method using Vapour Boron.

Whitaker and Company continues to flourish despite competition from aluminium and PVCu, firmly believing that timber is the only natural renewable material for manufacturing windows.

*Above: An aerial view of the works dating from October 1971. **Top:** A letterhead dating from 1908. **Left:** The works in the 1960s. **Facing page, top right:** A works dinner taken at the Little Bull in Denholme with Esau, standing (full profile) on the far left. **Facing page, centre left:** The second generation of the family; (from left) Mr. Jack, Mr. Harry and Mr. Fred. **Facing page, centre right:** John Whitaker demonstrating a machine in the 1950s. **Facing page, bottom left:** A Christmas dinner on 15th December 1952.*

Almost 200 years of Bradford history

Eighteen-twenty-five is the generally accepted and most often quoted date of the establishment of Samuel Dracup & Sons Ltd.

Samuel Dracup, born in 1793 was the grandson of Nathaniel Dracup who came from Idle and founded the Methodist movement in Great Horton in 1746.

Like his father and grandfather before him, Samuel was a shuttlemaker. He was ambitious and prospered so that the Dracup trustees could afford to build the firm's present premises, Lane Close Mill, in 1841 and extend it in 1847. Nearby Bartle Lane (formerly Cliffe Lane) was so called after John Bartle, the first tenant of the newly built mill.

Samuel took his sons into partnership as they grew up and left the business to them and his daughter, Maria, when he died in 1866. Thirty years after his death, there was family conflict over the inheritance. Much property formerly owned by the family was sold by auction but Lane Close Mill was retained

Samuel's business was Jacquard machine manufacture. The early Jacquards were made of wood and hand operated. Samuel built his first card cutting machine in 1833, his first card repeater in 1834 and his first Jacquard in 1838. He is known to have travelled to France to learn about the Jacquard machine.

The first power driven Jacquard in the Bradford area was installed at Bank Top Mills, now Ashley Mills but then owned by Thomas Ackroyd. He lived close by the present Hare and Hounds, then called the Stone Tables Inn.

Work continued along traditional lines until the second world war. When it was over the Dracups, having worked to drawings while on munitions work, started their drawing office in 1946. Five generations of the family worked in the company, but, the last member, Mr Charles Dracup, was killed whilst climbing near Aviemore in March 1976. After continuing well into his own retirement age, his father sold the company to Eltex in 1984.

Eltex of Sweden Ltd, manufacturers of the Electronic Weft Stop Motion, had acquired Samuel Dracup & Sons Limited with a view to introducing Electronics to Jacquards. They had already bought a shareholding in a firm making textile machinery accessories, Irvin Hudson Limited and it was decided from that time to move to more extensive premises to allow for future expansion. The move was made in 1976, to the Lustra Works.

In 1981, the Swedish Company of AB Winklecentrifuge, which was a wholly owned subsidiary of Eltex, was bought by Irvin Hudson Ltd. It moved to the UK and was renamed Wifug Ltd. They manufacture Laboratory Centrifuges and the majority of the engineering for the production of these units was and is

effected by Irvin Hudson. It was going to be far more economical to bring the company to the UK. Then the premises in Bradford would manufacture the Centrifuge and the marketing could be centralised.

In 1982 the name of the company was changed to Eltex of Sweden Ltd, with Irvin Hudson and Wifug becoming divisions of that company.

Above: A Double Wilton Carpet Jacquard. **Top:** A Cross Border Jacquard. **Top left:** A 300 hook capacity centre-shed Jacquard used in the woven label trade. **Left:** A piano type Card Cutting Machine. **Facing page, top:** Lane Close Mill, Great Horton taken from a letterhead from the turn of the century. **Facing page, bottom left:** A Peg and Lacehole Card Cutting Machine. **Facing page, bottom right:** A full Jacquard Harness which is weaving brocade.

Dewavrin - the 'tops' in wool trading

A. Dewavrin Ltd of 14, Mill Street, Topmakers, can trace their origins back to 1842 in the town of Tourcoing in France, where the headquarters of the international group is still located. The Bradford company was founded by Albert Maes in 1936 as Anselme Dewavrin Ltd., with its first office in the old Swan Arcade. The name was shortened to A. Dewavrin Ltd. in 1959.

In constant touch with world wool markets, Dewavrin's continued success is in providing quality wool tops with a first class service

for both the UK and overseas market. Their quality and competitiveness arises from investment in the most modern processing equipment and the application of stringent quality control at all times.

Tops of guaranteed and consistent quality can thus be assured.

Albert Maes came to Bradford in 1936, sent from the already long-established Dewavrin Group of Tourcoing in France. His business was wool-merchanting and his purpose was to set up a branch of his company in the pre-eminent wool trading centre of the world.

The date of the Bradford company's incorporation was July 6th of that year. Albert Maes remained managing director until 1967 and continued to take an active role in the company until his retirement in 1975.

Outside his involvement in the business Albert took a great interest in the civic life of the city, the subscription concerts at St George's Hall and Bradford Arts Club being just two examples. He married a local woman and continued to live in Bradford even after his retirement.

The company's links with its French parent , for obvious reasons, had to be severed in 1940 but were quickly re-established after the liberation of France.

The company occupied offices in Manor Buildings, Manor Row until March 1957, when it moved to its present premises in Mill Street. These premises, built in the early 1870s, are Grade II listed and situated in what is now a conservation area.

André Maes, Albert's nephew joined the company in the early 1950s, succeeding him as managing director in 1967 and remaining in charge until his retirement in 1982. André also succeeded his uncle as the French Consul in Bradford.

Although raw wool is still significant to their business, the name Dewavrin itself is world famous for the production of wool tops for both the worsted and woollen spinning industries. The group owns the third largest wool combing plant in the world and, being almost totally automated and completely pollution-free, it is also the most modern.

The Bradford company's main customers are woollen and worsted spinners in the United Kingdom and abroad, particularly the Republic of Ireland, Germany, Italy, France and Spain.

Above: The premises at 14, Mill Street. **Facing page, top:** *M. Albert Maes who first came to Bradford from the French parent company in 1936.*
Facing page, bottom right: *André Maes, Albert's nephew who succeeded him as managing director.*

Holmes Mann - a humble beginning that led to greater things

In 1890, Mr. Jonas Holmes and Mr. Matthew Mann moved into 202, Leeds Road, Bradford, ordered in nails, wood and paper and, recognising the potential of the site they occupied, remained in business there for 40 years. They had had experience in the packing case trade and soon had orders flowing in for their own business.

They decided early on to add rolling boards for cloth to their stock in trade and so became members of the Bradford Rolling Board and Packing Case Makers' Society. This association had very strict rules which had to be read and understood because no-one *will be allowed to plead ignorance in case of a breach thereof.*

If a member lost his copy it would cost him 3d for another one, a not inconsiderable sum in those days. The members' dues stood at 7d a week and if arrears exceeded eight shillings the man would be withdrawn from the shop. And his contributions were refused unless he brought along his card for them to be recorded.

The society allowed no boy over 16 to be taken on unless he had worked in the trade before. The men worked a standard fifty hour week, from 7 am until 5.30 pm with half an hour for breakfast and an hour for dinner. In 1905, a new rule was introduced: *One Boy will be allowed to work at Casemaking to every three men 20 years of age and over.*

In 1930, the business moved to its present location on Harris Street. During the war years it took orders from the Munitions Supply Company making boxes and grenade holders for them.

Presently they are suppliers to many industries including light engineering, food and the fabrics and plastics industries. Most of Holmes Mann's trade is with other local companies. They produce a large

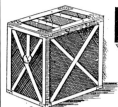

range of packaging products so that the customer can be offered a 'one-stop shop' solution to most of their packaging requirements.

The firm specialises in bespoke pallets, cases and combination packs. Several local companies produce some items that overlap with those of Holmes Mann but none of them produce the whole range.

The company has been set some interesting challenges over the years. In 1989, wooden packing cases with polystyrene fittings were made to transport portraits of HRH Prince Charles from Dean Clough in Halifax to London. Some years ago, Holmes Mann manufactured a huge and virtually flat packing case for a metal gasket which was used by Red Adair to extinguish a North Sea Oil rig fire. The largest packing case or crate within living memory was made to pack gas separators for Abu Dhabi. The crates were 40 feet long, 14 feet high and had to be assembled on site around the gas separators before getting a police escort to the docks.

The company's future plans include developing the production of printed tape and tubes, the winning of a greater share of the packaging machinery market and the installation of the environmental standard ISO 14001. The latter would be a rare achievement making Holmes Mann amongst the first packaging companies in Yorkshire to attain this.

Above: Matthew Mann, co-founder of the company which still bears his name.
Top: This letterhead was used during the 1960s.
Left: Messrs. Holmes and Mann always prided themselves on their ability to provide whatever the customer wanted. This price list dates from 1913 and the range was extensive for that period.
Facing page, bottom: This photograph dates from the early 1970s and shows a delivery driver reversing into the warehouse on Duncombe Way.
Facing page, top: Jonas Holmes.

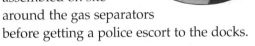

Bradford Property Trust - Triumph against all odds

Bradford Property Trust is that remarkable thing, a company which, over the last 70 years, has grown within an apparently contracting market. Its main activity is dealing and investing in tenanted residential property. The group is one of the largest listed property groups in the UK and probably the largest landlord in the private tenanted residential market.

It had a simple trading method of 'buying wholesale and selling retail'. It buys estates of tenanted residential property and sells those properties to owner-occupiers. The company now has a substantial portfolio of property for rent and owns in excess of 10,000 residential units throughout England and Wales.

BPT is in a position to manage its own properties rather than employing managing agents. This is an advantage not only because of cost efficiency but also because it gives the group close control over its own properties.

The properties are managed through six in-house teams based in four offices throughout Britain. The head office in Bradford co-ordinates financial and certain administrative functions of the group and the office at Epsom controls property management activities.

The company's size and experience enable it to look after individual property repairs and manage the complex accounts created by collecting rents, tenant moves and all aspects of tenancy agreements. The company liaises with tenants and contractors, managing vacant properties for selling or refurbishment before further letting.

The company has invested substantially in computer systems. They know the market well and continuously inspect and value properties for potential acquisition by private treaty and by auction.

Their portfolio of commercial properties is a small but significant part of their property assets.

Most good inspired ideas appear deceptively simple when explained. Likewise BPT's business

***Above:** Market Street Bradford, circa 1900.*

venture,'buying wholesale/selling retail'. It was strikingly and successfully original when its co-founder hit on the idea in the 1920s.

The company was founded in April 1928 but its roots go back to 1919 when a Bradford taxi driver brought Fred Gresswell into the property market. Gresswell was born in the Lincolnshire village of Digby in 1891, the fifth child of a farm labourer.

By the age of thirteen he was working full time as a

grocer's assistant. By the time war broke out in 1914 he had become an insurance salesman in Leeds, so that, after the war he set up as an insurance broker in Bradford's Swan Arcade. He rented his offices for £35 a year and scraped a living, partly by subletting them

for two hours each lunchtime! Earning less than £4 a week, he was surprised when a taxi driver neighbour made him a proposition. Would Gresswell sell his house for him as he didn't want his clients to know that he was leaving? The normal commission would be paid for this service.

Gresswell sold the house so quickly and obtained his £20 so easily that he decided forthwith to become an estate agent. He used his £20 to share larger offices in Bradford's Market Street with the Allied Textiles Industrial Council and made his agency slogan, 'Small Profits and Quick Returns'.

He did so well that the other local agents asked him to join their association. This meant accepting their code of practice and prevented the commission-cutting that had given Gresswell's firm its edge. Gresswell was already looking beyond simple agency work to speculative property dealing.

One transaction gave him a great deal of satisfaction. It made no profit but stimulated and amused him. He was a member of the Bradford Civic Society when St. George's Hall came up for sale. It was a building of great historical interest and had been offered to the City Council for £100,000. Although the price was reasonable they were unable to negotiate because of a shortage of money. It was owned by the Rank Organisation who had been using it as a cinema which they were now closing.

The Civic Society was asked to make a valuation with a view to raising the money privately and then to approach Mr Rank with the offer. The Civic Society, unable to find enough sponsors, wanted to withdraw. Gresswell's valuation was £35,000. He went himself to sort out matters with J. Arthur Rank, who pointed out that to build St. George's Hall at the time would cost £300,000, three times the asking price.

Gresswell replied that, in his experience, a building was only worth what it could be used for. As a road

planning scheme threatened to cut the building in half, it could only be used for warehouses. After thinking this over, Mr. Rank accepted Gresswell's estimate and sold it for £35,000. Gresswell passed on the Hall to the Council for the same price and considerably enhanced his own reputation.

Neither tenants nor building societies anticipated the mass movement from renting to owner occupation that was to transform residential property ownership over the next 50 years in the UK. Gresswell had no idea that he was to be a pioneer in that movement when he paid £95 each for sixteen houses in St. Stephen's Road, Bradford, but this deal was to be the blueprint for thousands of later sales by BPT.

Unlike Gresswell, Algernon Denham, the company's co-founder, had been involved in finance from the beginning of his career. Born in Brighouse in 1885, he began his career at sixteen earning £1 a week as a clerk.

In 1910 he joined the banking arm of the Halifax Permanent Building Society in Bradford, later becoming a Halifax director and manager of the Bradford branch of the Union Bank.

In 1928, the two men formed a £1,000 company which grew, even through the economic depression of the 30s, survived the war that destroyed much of its housing stock and expanded in the post-war market where private landlords became political punchbags.

After the formation of the company, Gresswell was able to close down his estate agency and become a full time property dealer. Backed by the financial resources of his fellow shareholders and the lines of credit available through the bank, he scoured lists of property auctions for suitable residential estates. There were few on offer in Bradford but London

Above: Fred Gresswell. ***Right:*** *The Anglo-South American Bank in Market Street, later to form part of Barclays Bank, pictured circa 1930.* ***Far right:*** *A 1930s plan of properties owned by BPT in Saltaire.*

landlords were packing the auction rooms. The company went there to bid.

In its early years, the company provided an essential middle ground between landlord and tenant. It enabled other landlords to relinquish the responsibilities of low yielding residential estates. Tenants were convinced that the novel idea of buying their own houses was not only possible but sensible. BPT sold on properties from the estates they had acquired to their tenants for a small profit. As the business grew, the necessity to realise a cash investment receded. Soon it was managing a large portfolio of residential property. From 1933 this began to include property in Saltaire.

Saltaire
The village of Saltaire is an outstanding example of the paternalism and far-sightedness of mill owners like Titus Salt, who obviously also meant it to be a memorial to himself. It is undoubtedly one of the finest industrial villages of its type in Britain. Covering 25 acres it had 22 streets, 850 houses, hospital, school, park, baths, Sunday school, wash-houses, railway station and Salt's huge mill. Compared with the state of things in other parts of Bradford, workers felt very thankful to be able to live there.

Salt built it in the third quarter of the 19th century, intending it not only as a workplace but somewhere that supplied all his workers' needs.
The streets were named after Salt's relatives.
A worker's position in the mill determined which street he lived in. Albert Road was for managers, George Street for overseers and so on. The name of the village is a combination of Salt's own name and

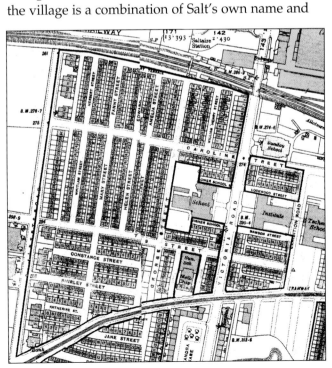

that of the river that runs past.

In 1933, BPT bought the whole village which had increased to 964 houses from Salts (Saltaire) Ltd. for £164,500, the equivalent of just £100 a house. The company had to spend a further £100,000 repairing and modernising before resale.

According to a conveyance of October 6th 1933, the first property sold by BPT (No. 5 Gordon Terrace) was conveyed to a Mrs. Phyllis Brookes. Some houses were sold to sitting tenants who became owner occupiers. The most recent conveyance in that area from BPT was in September 1991.

The war years

In 1939 the company braced itself for the destruction of its residential estates but the 'phoney war' went on for nearly a year and business continued as usual. Housing prices had slumped when war was declared and BPT bought cautiously. The maintenance of their existing estates became a serious problem after the introduction of wartime building licenses. Conversions and modernisation had to be shelved and even essential repairs were difficult. Licenses were virtually impossible to obtain for work not directly connected with the war effort and materials and skilled labour were in short supply.

In 1940 came the first heavy bombing. It was impossible to insure property against war damage, but the government stepped in and accepted responsibility for all claims. The compensation money received from them enabled BPT to start on their massive backlog of house repairs once the war was over.

It was during the war years with BPT's concerns about the huge cost of rebuilding houses damaged by the Blitz that Fred Reddihough, head of a Yorkshire wool business, agreed to buy a one third share of BPT.

Although the housing market had collapsed during the war, the company had completed a number of small residential property deals outside London. There had been very little competition for houses in the main industrial centres while they were prime bombing targets, but, in March 1944 BPT bought a 257-house estate in Stockton on Tees for £45,000, just £177 each.

The end of the war brought a new phase in the company's history. It had to grow to survive and growing brought new faces to the board room and larger deals through the books. The largest of their immediately post war purchases was the 625-house Hull Garden Village.

This had been built at the beginning of the century by the Reckitt family (joint owners of the Reckitt and Colman group). The family had decided to sell its investment and re-invest more profitably. The

established the company's expertise in working with local communities.

During the forties and fifties, the group traded in agricultural land, notably the 15,600-acre Rufford Abbey Estate and the 7,420-acre Brightwell Estate at Ipswich, including the RAF airfield at Martlesham. After the RAF gave it up in the 1960s, during the 1970s and 1980s BPT developed an award-winning 1,200-home village and the Group is still involved in the development of some housing in the village.

In the Spring of 1963, when BPT launched its shares on the stock market, it had accumulated a portfolio of 5,877 houses and 439 flats. BPT's stock market début was not a success. Only 28% of the shares on offer were taken up by investors, and in 1963 that ranked as a failure for a new issue from a property company.

This early set-back was only temporary and very soon BPT continued its development and growth. Started 70 years ago with an inspired idea from Fred Gresswell, the financial acumen of Algernon Denham and the subsequent financial support of Fred Reddihough, BPT today is a major property company. Listed on the London Stock Exchange with a capitalisation of over £400 million, it owns in excess of 10,000 residential properties.

Trading in people's homes is a very complex and emotive business. Every balance sheet entry represents someone's home and every purchase and every sale has a direct impact on someone's life. There is no simple formula for operating profitably yet sympathetically.

BPT feel they have managed to steer a successful course between social responsibility and financial profit. The company has made history by helping to break the established order that landlords must own and tenants must rent.

transaction brought BPT back into the headlines and a flood of further estate propositions were made. During the 1950s, garden village estates established in the early 1900s became an important source of investment and dealing. Management of these

Top left: Algernon Denham, co-founder of BPT. **Centre:** *St George's Hall, purchased in a remarkable deal by Fred Gresswell, seen here in its wartime role as a cinema.*

The story of 'Mr Bradford & Mr Bingley'

In the years following the Industrial Revolution, in the centres of the textile industry in Yorkshire, workers left their remote cottages and came to live in clusters around the mills where there was work to be had. It began to be realised that the savings of one group could provide the loans required by another, so that buying their houses became a not unreasonable ambition for mill workers in steady employment.

The Bradford Equitable was the second earliest building Society to be formed in Bradford, after the Bradford Union. It held its first meeting at the Mechanics' Institute in 1846, prospered steadily, and by the early 1960s, led by its chairman at the time, Mr. Walter James, had amassed assets of £52 million.

Bingley, slightly more rural with one third of its population still engaged in farming in the first half of the 19th century, still felt the impact of the new industrialisation. There too, small groups of

savers formed similar societies and, in 1871, various of these enterprises joined to form the Bingley, Morton, Shipley & Keighley Permanent Benefit Building Society. By 1962, after similar steady growth, its assets of £41 million rivalled Bradford's. The Bingley Society's general manager, Mr. Bob Gardner, wanted his society to be in the list of the top ten societies and looked for the merger with a similarly sized society that would be necessary to fulfil his ambition.

The society we know today was first conceived in a private conversation between Messrs James and Gardner after a meeting of the Yorkshire County Association of Building Societies, hosted by the Leeds Permanent Building Society at its headquarters on the Headrow. Many meetings later the Bradford & Bingley came into being and proved to be just as good an idea as it founders had forecast.

the millennium is proving to be competition in the market for mortgages and savings. It prides itself on offering a safe place for its clients' savings, on being a wise counsellor to customers seeking financial advice and an obliging investor in those

wishing to better their fortunes through loans to buy their own property. The Bradford & Bingley is a mutual society with no shareholders to pay so that they can put their customers first. Using their experience of the last forty years, they intend their march into the 21st century to be an exhilarating one.

Above: An advertisement of 1951. *Centre:* A view of the Aire Valley and Bingley taken from Gilstead Moor with the Society's former head office middle right. *Facing page, top right:* Forster Square, Bradford in 1891. *Facing page, bottom left:* The first floor offices of Bradford Equitable's Bank Street premises. *Facing page, bottom right:* A cover from some contemporary advertising literature. *Below:* Main Street, Bingley around 1900.

A decade of small mergers with other local societies left the new society looking for acquisitions on a larger scale. Twenty years after the Bradford Bingley merger, Bob Gardner retired, having seen the society's assets increase from £30 million to an unimaginable £3,430 million.

The biggest challenge for the Bradford & Bingley in the ten years leading up to

Grattan plc - the story so far.....

Grattan was established as a retail jeweller by John Fattorini in 1912. Success and rapid expansion led to the purchase of warehouse premises on Grattan Road, from which the company gets its name. It added drapery and footwear to its range of goods, then sold by catalogue to reach a broader customer base. Local agents were recruited to take orders and deliver

parcels on commission. The most amusing so far is for one bra and one hammer, marked 'Urgent, wanted for wedding'!

The Second World War brought the complication of 'coupons'. Each garment had a coupon value and each customer had a coupon allocation. Just as the 1948/49 winter catalogue was printed, the Board of Trade made wide relaxations in the coupon regulations and a list of alterations had to be inserted in each copy.

The company's in-house magazine,

Spotlight, for 1964, describes how the catalogues were produced at that time. It was printed, 16 pages at once, on large machines. Dates when the merchandise had to be ready for the photographer were worked out. On the due dates, buyers who had

selected their ranges handed over new samples. On occasion, the process was delayed, reasons for lateness varied from the weather spoiling outdoor shots to a cat falling into the developing tank!

The photographs were arranged and checked, then accurate layouts were made so the photo-engraver could make printing plates. All the printing colours were made up of yellow, blue, red and black. Through a magnifying glass, dots of these could be seen in the fawns and greens of the garments. Royal blue was particularly difficult to produce.

Engravers also had their stories to tell; one had negatives spoilt by a spider making a web across the camera lens. Eventually, the colour proof was rushed, (Dr Beeching permitting), by train to the catalogue department where it was checked before printing. Meanwhile the type matter was set. The actual publication of a catalogue was late only once in the history of the firm- during the printing strike of 1959.

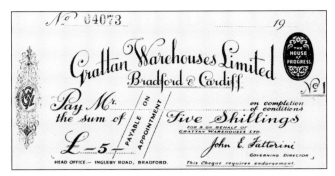

Spotlight told the workforce in the mid-sixties about the firm's acquisition of a computer. It was felt necessary to insert, 'A computer is a machine which can be arranged to do many kinds of work.'!

In the early '80s 'Personal' shopping was introduced with Grattan Direct and Manorgrove was set up as a retail discount outlet. In 1981 Kaleidoscope and Scotcade came under the Grattan banner, strengthening the direct response business. In 1985 came the merger with Next plc and the launch of Next Directory. Simultaneously, plans were finalised for the new Listerhills Warehouse.

In 1991 the partnership with Next was dissolved when the business was sold to the world's largest mail order company, Otto Versand. The latter company comprises 38 companies in 16 countries in 3 continents with 54,000 employees worldwide. Grattan is in sympathy with Versand's maxim, 'To stand still is to stagnate.'

Within the UK, Grattan's is the fourth largest home shopping company and claims to be the most up-market of the 'Big 5'. There are two 1,000 plus page catalogues, Grattan and Look Again, which has unique young fashion merchandise and is targeted at the fashion-conscious. The majority of customers for both brands are agents who receive 10% commission on their payments.

Grattan also has has two direct Home Shopping brands (the fastest-growing sector in mail order). The

first is Kaleidoscope whose core offer is a unique range of fashion aimed at 35-55 year old women supported by a stylish home textile and kitchen ware offer. The second direct brand is Curiosity Shop, specialising in fun and innovative gadgets, gifts and other household products.

Recent achievements include an expansion of the personal courier delivery service to 90% of all deliveries. 'Hanging Garments' now accounts for 10%

of deliveries, which has improved the appearance of clothes when they are received. Improvements have been made in the cleaning and restoring of returned goods and investment has been made in the order entry and customer services call centre.

Facing page, far left: Two catalogues dating from different decades, the 1930s (top) and the 1960s (bottom). Facing page, bottom left: A 1962 advertisement from the catalogue, with the ever-present flannelette nighties! Facing page, top right: This picture of the Grattan premises was taken from a letterhead dating from 1934. Facing page, bottom right: Long before the days of high-tech design aids, graphic artists had to 'paste-up' their designs. This was often a long, laborious task and involved equipment such as wax guns and scalpels. Top left: In the 1950s and 60s agents of the catalogue were paid with

cheques such as this, which were redeemable when their sales had reached a certain figure. Above, left: Measuring out cloth which would be dispatched to the agent. Above: A hand made pram, one of many sold from the factory. Right: The Inspection Room.

Success through change for Whaleys of Bradford

This company was established in 1869 by Mr. Samuel Whaley, about whom not a great deal more is known. The activities of his enterprise at that time were silk and jute weaving, with one floor processing textile sacks and bags.

The original premises were off Leeds Road, before moving to India Mills in Bolton Road in1908, finally taking over its present site, Harris Court Mills in 1973.

Whaleys can, with some justification, call themselves a family firm, since Harry Jowett, who took over the reins in 1900, was the grandfather of the present managing director.

During the First World War, weaving was suspended and silk making abandoned. When normal work recommenced an industrial fabric section was established to furnish the textile finishing industry.

Just before Harry Jowett's death in 1921, the firm was taken over by his two sons in law, Fred Popplewell (MD) and James Robert McIlvenny and after the last war, Joined by the sons of James

Robert, i.e. Harry and James Fredrick, who is currently managing director, assisted by his son and director, Peter, now representing the fourth generation.

Over the years the company has expanded and diversified. It has introduced a department which specialises in producing theatre curtains along with a range of flame-proofed fabrics in addition to a large fashion fabric section supplying fabric designers direct, with a separate mail order

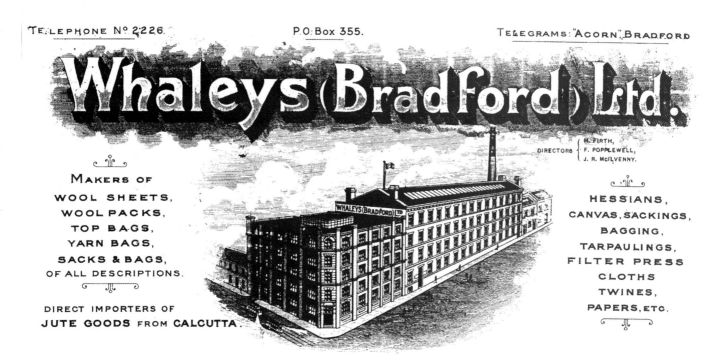

TELEPHONE Nº 2226.   P.O. Box 355.   TELEGRAMS: "ACORN" BRADFORD

Whaleys (Bradford) Ltd.

DIRECTORS { H. FIRTH, F. POPPLEWELL, J. R. McILVENNY.

MAKERS OF
WOOL SHEETS,
WOOL PACKS,
TOP BAGS,
YARN BAGS,
SACKS & BAGS,
OF ALL DESCRIPTIONS.

DIRECT IMPORTERS OF
JUTE GOODS FROM CALCUTTA.

HESSIANS,
CANVAS, SACKINGS,
BAGGING,
TARPAULINGS,
FILTER PRESS
CLOTHS
TWINES,
PAPERS, ETC.

COTTON & CANVAS WRAPPERS   ROLLER COVERINGS USED BY DYERS, FINISHERS & LAUNDRIES.

INDIA MILLS.

company. It is interesting to note that this includes offering silk again, after an absence of 70 years!

The Sewing Factory manufactures all the types of bags for the textile and coal industries.

Currently, over fifty per cent of the company's products are exported world-wide, particularly to North America and Europe.

The management is almost as well-known for its sporting prowess as it is for its

Whaleys is a company that has seen many changes and in fact implemented many itself in order to grow. It is this diversity and foresight that will lead it well into he next century.

Above and left: The above picture dates from 1994 and the one on the left from 1944, showing the re-flooring of the old mill dam. Whaleys premises have been extensively renovated and these pictures show the difference between the building then and now. **Facing page, bottom:** *A letterhead dating from 1920, showing the premises on Bolton Road.* **Facing page, top left:** *(Left) James McIlvenny and Peter James (right) with the family founder, Harry Jowett in the picture behind.* **Below:** *A family picture comprising all the present directors.*

company's products. Mr. Harry Jowett played Rugby Union for Bradford, whilst James (Jimmy) McIlvenny was a professional soccer player with Bradford City. Fred Popplewell was a well known cricketer in the Bradford League. Harry McIlvenny played amateur soccer for Park Avenue and England, and hockey was the sport of both James and Peter, representing Bradford and later Ben Rhydding.

It seems fitting therefore that Whaleys should have a sporting company secretary, John Rawnsley, who specialises in cyclocross, and who not only inaugurated the fearsome 3 Peaks Annual 37 years ago, but still organises and participates in it today.

The company with 'bags' of experience

At the turn of the century, when brown paper carrier bags were made by hand and had their string handles put on using glue and a brush, Robert Crooke was working in the paper trade. His son, Rowland Sunderland Crooke was well grounded in the business when in 1912, in premises in Leeds Road, Bradford, he set up his company. Its main activity at first was the buying and cutting of paper to sell locally.

By 1913, his turnover had reached £5,500. To begin with, Rowland Crooke saw all customers personally, though later he had to employ 5 travellers. 1929 was a bumper year when he took 5,260 orders in person and new customers averaged one every day. He was proud of his record as an employer and made it a rule to pay higher wages than the Board of trade rates. He was amply compensated for this in the loyalty and unbroken service records of his employees.

By 1930 there were ten staff on the road. Most of the paper used was from Scandinavia and

continued to be until the 1980s 'Buy British' campaign. In 1955, the business was taken over by R.P. Crooke, grandson of the founder. In the sixties he purchased the premises at Idle Road, supplying throughout the North of England and expanding the production of paper bags. Before that, bags had been bought in for resale. This move forward was marked by the formation of the Dependable Paper Bag Co Ltd. In 1964 G.T.

Whitehead Ltd was purchased. The same year brought the move to the premises on Idle Road which, by coincidence, were built in the same year the original firm was founded. In 1968 the business was further enlarged when it absorbed the paper bag business of Harry B. Berry Ltd.

The Diamond Jubilee of the company was celebrated in 1972 with a dinner at the Bankfield Hotel in Bingley., at which gold watches were presented to three women who between them had served the company for 75 years. A Miss G.

Landon, who had put in 40 years' service, had retired the previous year.

In 1976, the founder's grandson, Peter Crooke, died, his son Paul succeeded him as chairman at the tender age of 21. The work of the office staff was fully computerised in 1980. Business continued to increase until, in 1994 warehousing and distribution was transferred to a 10-acre site at Friar's Industrial Estate. The

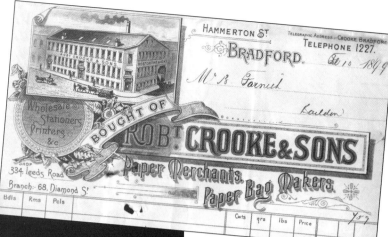

packaging in modern materials. They have large stocks of all their products. Their own sheeting plant enables paper to be cut to customer's requirements.

The present chairman, Paul Rowland Crooke, together with company secretary, Jonathan Michael Crooke, seem set to lead the company through a fourth generation and into another century.

*Above: An invoice dating from 1919. **Facing page, bottom left:** A charming 1940s picture with the factory of the day in the background. **Facing page, top left:** Founder of the company, Mr Rowland Sunderland Crooke. **Centre:** The assembled staff outside the factory in the 1940s. **Below and below left:** The modern warehouse at Idle Road.*

company, still a family concern, began trading nationally. 1995 brought the merger with Osmond Hartley of Leeds.

Today, modern machinery ensures that Crookes' can economically produce orders both large and small. As well as paper bags, they supply polythene carriers and a range of modern

From the 'dark satanic mills' to the factories of Europe

When the Ovenden Worsted Spinning Company in Halifax closed down in 1904, Mr. Benson Turner lost his job there as general manager. However he was a man not easily daunted and he looked on this misfortune as a new beginning. He set up a business, together with his elder son, Wilfred to do worsted spinning

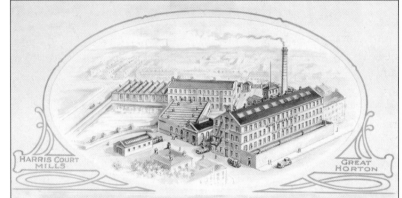

HARRIS COURT MILLS

GREAT HORTON

of Botany wool at Cliffe Mills, Great Horton. Part of the Ovenden company's work force moved with him, and, a short time later, his brother Herbert and his uncle, Arthur Turner, also joined the business.

It prospered, with each member of the family having his own area of responsibility. Benson ran the mill, and Herbert sold yarn. Wilfred, Benson's son took charge of buying the wool after he had left Hanson Grammar School and studied the latest wool techniques in Hamburg. Wilfred succeeded his father as chairman of the firm and remained in this position until his death in 1956.

In 1916 Station Mills at Wyke were acquired and equipped to produce high quality West Riding cloth. When, in the same year, the

original mill at Great Horton was destroyed by fire, Wilfred Turner bought Harris Court Mill which has operated ever since. Wilfred believed in progress and took every opportunity to expand his premises and his list of customers. The company's prosperity

continued until the second world war. The mills were still busy during this period but now they made yarns for uniforms, mainly military clothing, with just the balance made available for home trade.

Up to 1946 the business had operated with just two mills. However, because of a labour shortage in West Yorkshire after the war, some of the machinery was transported to Lutterworth near Leicester and there was a spinning unit there until 1962. It was closed then because of improvements in spinning technology and an increase in the production of acrylics which made the Lutterworth machinery redundant. New machinery installed in Bradford meant that the company's production level was maintained. The company now entered the electronic age, under Benson Turner, grandson of the founder. who had become joint managing director with his cousin Reg Turner and his brother in law Max Sutcliffe.

In 1964 Harris Court was re-organised and equipped for the second time. The multi-storey buildings there were sold and the single-storey ones were converted to deal solely with acrylic yarns for machine knitting. The newly-installed Prince-Smith machinery ran for 24 hours a day and produced 27,000 pounds of yarn a week.

1965 brought the major decision to set up the company's own dyeing facility. The textile industry supplies the world of fashion which is a very volatile market. If trends are not picked up immediately and yarns in the latest colours not in supply quickly enough, business is lost to rivals.

After discussions with Norman Wood and Sons, the two companies jointly financed the formation of Turner and Wood (Dyers) Ltd., which would co-

ordinate spinning, dyeing and winding within one supplier. Knitters could now deal with one firm.

Between 1974 and 1979, in further necessary moves to keep up with the market, two and a quarter million pounds was invested in new spinning and dyeing machinery and building work. Now the three factories retain only the names of 'dark satanic mills'. The buildings are actually large, modern, single-storey units, close to the open countryside, providing a clean working environment. The by-gone clatter and rattle has become a quiet hum and the fibre-laden air has been replaced by air-conditioning.

The company's products are supplied to machine knitting businesses in the UK who supply chain stores and specialist retailers. In the UK the main markets are the East Midlands, Leicester and Nottingham. Goods are dispatched abroad to most of Europe and the Middle East.

Above: A staff celebration in the 1940s. **Facing page, bottom left:** *Mr Wilfred Turner, joint founder of the company.* **Facing page, centre:** *Harris Court Mills at Great Horton.* **Below:** *Benson Turner staff in the 1920s. Mr Turner is in the centre of the picture.*

Five generations of good old fashioned service

I n 1867, in the terraced house beside the Liberal Club in Towngate, Wyke, Josh Ellis, the great-great uncle of the present proprietor set up his butcher's shop. The shop was equipped as a slaughterhouse and, in those days, was not open on a Monday as that was the day for the slaughtering of animals. For the rest of the week it became a shop where the meat was cut up and sold.

Several years later a slaughterhouse was built in Brick Row, the street behind Town Gate. Josh was a clever butcher who knew that anything he had to throw away was his loss. He

had a marble slab and a cellar in which to keep his meat cool and dry. An ice box was introduced in the cellar in 1920 and a refrigerator in the shop in the mid 1930s.

The shop, from a very early time delivered meat throughout the district to many of the larger houses of mill owners, dye house owners, doctors and other professional people. The earliest deliveries were on foot, then by pony and trap, then bicycle. By the late forties motor transport had arrived in the shape of a Jowett van.

James Stainthorpe, a nephew, joined the business in the latter years of the 19th century, followed by his nephew, Frank Stobart in the early 1920s. Frank took over the business in 1928. The business continued at these premises until 1963, though there was obviously much modernising of equipment and surroundings. The war brought rationing and consequently the closing of the slaughterhouse. The killing of stock was centralised to ensure fair shares and in the 1950s when rationing of meat ended, the slaughterhouse was not reopened but converted for the purpose of meat preparation and manufactured products. The next generation of the family in the person of Mr. Kenneth Stobart became a partner in the 1950s. In 1963 the business moved just a mile to Carr Lane. When the STOPAK label was extended to cover prepacked meat, most of the major stores in Bradford and Leeds were supplied. Amongst these

were Busby's, Brown Muff's, Jesse Stephenson, Lewis's and Lion Stores, all, of course, long gone and replaced by supermarkets

Stobarts have served the Bradford community -and recently far beyond . Over a period of 130 years they have had good reason to pride themselves on their service, their quality and their price.

*Above: A replica of the original delivery vehicle. **Left:** Mr Frank Stobart (right) and his assistant, Alan Rhodes in 1948. **Facing page, top:** Preparing sausages in the 1960s. **Facing page, centre:** The distribution point for Stobarts' quality products in the 1960s. **Facing page, bottom left:** Pie production in the 1960s. The standards were very good at the time but were far from those required today. **Facing page, bottom right:** An assortment of products in the Sto-Pak label in the 1960s. Today faggots are a very popular line. In the old days the same recipe was known as Savoury Duck and was sold hot on Saturday nights as the shoppers went home. **Below:** The meat preparation department around 1965.*

Today, Stobarts' main markets are wholesale distributors and retail outlets on the continent as well as in the UK. They produce their own-label packaging for supermarkets, for such products as pies, faggots, burgers and ready-meals. The business has diversified but continues under the registered title 'STO-PAK' and the company promises deliveries anywhere, anytime.
Mr. Kenneth's sons Andrew and Neil had joined the company in the 80s. For five generations

Thomas Wright - part of the city's industrial scene for almost a century-and-a-half

Founded by Thomas Wright in 1850, the great grandfather of present MD Mr TE 'Teddy' Wright, the company's primary function was to manufacture and supply washers for spinning and roving machines used in the textile trade in Yorkshire. This product range gradually expanded to include many items used regularly in textile mills and dyehouses.

The advent of the motor car at the turn of the century brought with it new opportunities for many including Thomas Wright. Using existing methods

applied to the new market, the company began manufacturing washers and oil seals for the burgeoning car industry. Between the 1930's and the 50's the company developed to become a leading Motor Factor and Mill Furnishing enterprise.

The late 50's brought with it the first signs of things to come. Through their existing factoring businesses the Wrights had built up strong connections with industrial air compressors.

This led, at one stage, to the firm actually manufacturing air compressors under the now familiar THORITE trade

name of the Thomas Wright Thorite Group. These were sold to textile machinery manufacturers who exported them along with their own machinery.

It was in fact Teddy Wright, the present MD who instigated the move into pneumatics, his interest in things mechanical led quite naturally into this field once he had seen the potential for this relatively new technology in the developing industries of post war Britain.

It was at this time that Mr Roger Bate came onto the scene. Roger was a representative for a company called Benton and Stone. Benton and Stone were the originators and manufacturers of the famous Enots tubing fittings. Roger had approached Teddy Wright with a view to Thomas Wrights stocking a few fittings in order to "help out" a few of Benton and Stone's local customers. One thing led to another and Roger's persuasive selling techniques soon saw a range of air service equipment, valves and cylinders on Thomas Wrights shelves at Bower Street, Bradford.

It wasn't too long of course before other compressed air equipment manufacturers also noticed the success which Thomas Wrights were enjoying with local Yorkshire industry. They were not slow in spotting a

Above: The Bower Street mill department. The men are making felt washers for the textile industry for use on their spinning and roving machines. This was the core of Thomas Wright's business at one time but it has since diversified. *Top right:* The Bower Street premises in the 1950s. *Right:* An early delivery van in the motor factoring days. Hepolite was a trade name for a range of locally manufactured pistons sold by the company.

good thing and began making approaches to the company. One of them happened to be a company called CA Norgren who manufactured a range of air processing equipment under licence from the parent company in the USA. A deal was struck and Thomas Wrights became a Norgren Stockist, thereby forging a historical link that exists to this day.

The achievements made at Bradford prompted Teddy Wright to open the Group's first "satellite" branch in Leeds, to be known as Thorite Pneumatics Ltd. The new company was set up in 1960 in premises on West Street, central Leeds. Tom Taylor of Thomas Wright

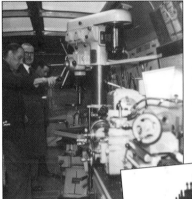

Bradford became "Director on the spot" at Leeds while Roger Bate continued his employment at Benton and Stone, helping out in his spare time in a consultative role at Thorite.

In November 1963 Mr Keith Dalton joined the company with initial responsibilities as Office Manager.

After four years service Keith accepted a Directorship of Thorite Pneumatics. This came about due to a move by Tom Taylor back to Bradford, where he assumed the mantle of Sales Director.

Keith is still with Thorite Ltd (the Pneumatics title has been dropped). He is now MD of Thorite Ltd as well as holding Directorships of Thomas Wright Air Centres Ltd, Thomas Wright North West Ltd. and Comprite Ltd.

Although Teddy Wright may not have realised it at the time, the opening of Thorite Pneumatics was to set the pattern for the development of the Pneumatics Industry through distribution. This is exemplified in the Thomas Wright - Thorite Group being Norgren's largest independent distributor in the UK. The infrastructure necessary to achieve this has been built on the Company's unswerving dedication to Customer Service.

In order to achieve this a strategy of continual expansion across the North of England has been adhered to. The company now has a total of nine branches serving its customer base with off the shelf products as well as providing in depth knowledge and expertise of the products. Thomas Wright Bradford remains the controlling influence of the Group.

Brand loyalty is an inherent part of the culture of Thomas Wright and applies to most products marketed by the company not just Norgren Products. The support of suppliers like Norgren is greatly appreciated by the company and particularly in an age where the Distributor has an ever more important role to play in the future of industry.

It is the company's breadth and depth of expertise and deep seated involvement in the industry which will provide the means for it to move successfully forward into the next century.

The strong historical relationship between the Thomas Wright - Thorite Group and Norgren should help strengthen the new initiative and cement good relationships between them and their customers.

With a history full of challenge and change, the future looks bright for the Group.

*Above (**both pictures**): A mobile exhibition of the company's products from the 1950s. **Top right**: An industrial exhibition from the 1960s. **Right**: The premises on Chapman Street as they are today.*

A century and a half at Albion Mill

Scott (Dudley Hill) Ltd. was founded by Silas Scott, son of Walter Scott, principal of the Airedale College at Undercliffe. Silas left school at 13 and worked for Milligan, Forbes & Co., a progressive firm of cloth merchants. In 1850, when he was 24, he set up on his own in premises in Bridge Street. By 1866 he had purchased Albion Mill at Dudley Hill, installed some secondhand looms and was manufacturing his own cloth. Cloth is still being woven there 137 years on.

Silas Scott did not neglect his duties as a citizen. He was a town councillor from 1863 until 1874 and, at the time of his death in 1909, he was senior magistrate of the city. He was the last magistrate in Bradford to condemn a man to the stocks for drunkenness, reviving the disused punishment because "it merely hurt the culprit himself and did not injure the man's wife and children."

Between 1874 and 1894 severe tariffs made exporting to Europe and America unprofitable, but the company was in good heart when Silas's only son, Walter, took over Albion Mill in 1891. At that time it contained 328 looms, valued at under £3,000. (In 1997 just one new loom is worth at least £50,000.) Fabrics were woven from wool, silk and cotton and Scotts' casement cloth was used to make cabin curtains for Cunard liners. (Today they make knee blankets for airlines.)

Walter's son, Val, ran the company from 1919 until his death in 1957, assisted by his own sons, Derek and Cedric. In 1925 a fire damaged goods worth several thousand pounds. This may have been the reason why Albion Mill was one of the first in Bradford to switch over from gas to electric lighting in 1928. The working week then was 52 and a half hours. Employees were granted one week of unpaid holiday in August and two days, also unpaid, at Christmas and Easter.

In the early 1930s the slump that was crushing British industry almost destroyed Scotts. When a factory inspector insisted the weaving shed must be painted the directors purchased a job lot of cheap paint and did the work themselves. There was no money left to buy yarn to weave or to pay wages. However, a customer was found who wanted weaving capacity and who provided his own yarn. Gradually the company switched from manufacturing on its own account to manufacturing on commission.

If this venture was to succeed, modern, efficient machinery had to be obtained. The banks would not lend money for investment of this sort, but Derek's wife was able to finance new, automatic Northrop looms, so Scotts was back in business.

The second world war brought a demand for uniform cloth. Val ran the business while his sons were in the Services.

Re-equipping continued after the war. By 1947 all the looms were automatic and an additional weaving shed was built. A dance hall at Hemsworth near Wakefield was purchased where 100 women were employed in burling and mending. The factory produced plain fabrics for menswear.

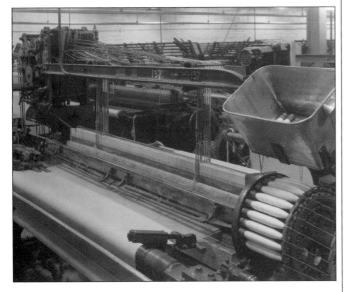

By 1965 the Northrop looms had been replaced by Saurers from Switzerland which in turn gave way to technically advanced Sulzers. These were faster and able to produce fancy cloths and the coveted name edge selvedges. Confidence was high.

In 1953, Derek's son, Michael, had joined the company, and from 1981, Michael's son, Adam, represented the 6th generation of the Scott family to play his part in the business. Adam introduced the computer with all its advantages to Albion Mills.

During the recession of the eighties, 45 of the 174 employees had to be made redundant and 16 of the 81 looms sold off. Again the company survived by the skin of its teeth. It was not until 1990 that eight new Dornier looms could be purchased, followed by a modern warping mill. Derek died in 1991, having devoted 64 years to the firm.

The company now runs 78 looms and the associated winding, warping, loom-preparation and mending departments. A wide range of fabrics is produced, haute couture, luxury suitings, plain menswear cloth, furnishing weight woollens and cottons to name but a few. Scotts' customers sell worldwide and the company seeks to provide the high levels of technical skill, flexibility and service they need.

All the pictures on these pages date from the Second World War.

Facing page, top and centre left: Warp twisting.
Facing page, centre right: The office.
Facing page, bottom right: Winding.
Above: The winding department.
Above left: A Northrop loom.
Left: The weaving department.
Below: Burling and mending to remove knots and faults before cloth is despatched to the finishers.

At the shops

Main picture: A rare and very atmospheric photograph, thought to date from before 1937 as Busby's had yet to extend into the premises of the Girls' Grammar School at the right hand (north) end of the property. Ultimately their premises extended beyond Hallfield Road into the building with the two pyramid-topped turrets. This is a real gem of a picture for anyone interested in nostalgia in general and bygone Bradford in particular. Pictures like this one are always better when the subjects in them are unaware that they are being photographed, as seems to be the case here. The excellent composition of the scene gives a good impression of what a busy street in Bradford would have been like, and the variety of cars and trucks in the picture adds even more character to the image. The Theatre Royal, built in 1865, was converted into a cinema in 1921 and closed in 1974. We can just see its canopy which extended over the footway of Manningham Lane. This canopy, on cast-iron columns, was replaced by a cantilevered version well before the 1950s. Sadly, the whole building is now demolished. The picture shows that at this time the carriageway was paved with granite setts, apart from the area between the tram rails which appears to be covered with asphalt. Trams would still have been running to Cross Flatts when this picture was taken.

Below: Manningham Lane seen in 1946 from the Yorkshire Penny Bank, at the spot formerly known as 'Pipers Grave.' From left to right we see Greenwoods outfitters - from little acorns great oak trees grow - the oak tree is their trade mark. The Regent Cinema with its faience facade opened in 1914, becoming the Essoldo in 1950 and later being demolished to make way for the ring road. After the sweet shop and chemists and Drewton Street we come to Busby's Store - a Bradford favourite if ever there was one. Formerly the Royal Arcade it became Busbys' from 1930. On the right hand side is the building containing the offices of the Independent Order of Rechabites also demolished for the ring road, this time the Hamm Strasse.

W.S..

Left: Looking more like a glamourous ocean liner than a department store, Busbys' took on a magnificent appearance when seen lit up on a cold wet night in 1938. The art-deco style was particularly suited to being lit up by flood-lights in this manner (not a common sight when this picture was taken) and the management of the store was proud of the claim that the electricity for the lamps was provided by the firm's own generator. This photograph records a view taken from the Hallfield Road side. The ground-floor windows each have a tastefully-organised window display showing various household scenes. Keen eyes may just be able to reveal the prams and baby department on the first floor, on the right of the picture.

Right: The full range of services available at Busbys' Manningham Lane store included gentlemans' hairdressing as well as the better known facilities available for ladies. Of course, on the gentlemans' side the services included shaving, beard trimming, moustache waxing and hair dyeing. We can only guess at the treatment given to this famous old customer. The photograph was one of several taken for publicity purposes. This picture brings back memories of trips to traditional barbers shops, in the days before unisex hairdressers began to eat into their trade. Most men will remember their first trip to the barber's shop as a four or five year old. Barbers would be used to putting the minds of their little customer at rest by sitting them on a hassock or cushion and taking a great interest in the youngster's preferred style.

Below: Space was clearly at a premium in the manicure section of Busbys' Beauty Parlour when this picture was taken. The scene dates back to a time when ladies were very secretive about their personal beauty arrangements. More mature ladies will recall the days when there were individual cubicles at the hairdressers. What went on behind that curtain (in terms of perming and colouring) was strictly between the client and the hairdresser; it would be impolite to ask if a friend's hair had been subjected to a particular treatment - and unknown to admit to one!

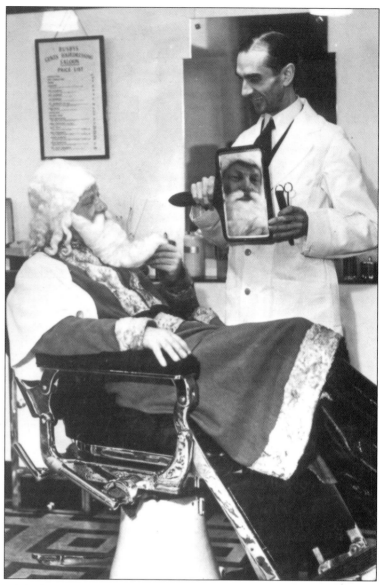

to a sign noticed in the window, it reads " Free off ration Soap Powders 3d, 4d, 11d... no coupon required. " Rationing was introduced to Britain in 1940, initially on butter, sugar and bacon. It was later extended to cover other foodstuffs, meat in March 1941 and cheese in May the same year. Clothing too was subject to tight controls and constant shortages.

Top: A sea of faces smile for the camera at a Busbys' home appliance demonstration in the late 1930s. The articles being shown include a gas cooker, an electric breakfast

Above: A wartime shopping scene from the 1940s featuring a corner shop on the outskirts of the town centre. "Open all hours" could be the title of the photograph if we went in for that kind of thing... it certainly looks like the corner- shop featured in the popular television comedy. We noticed the delivery bike propped-up against the wall at the side of the shop. Delivery services abounded at this time, and of course, there was seldom need to lock your bike up when left unattended. Our wartime reference relates

cooker and a variety of devices designed to assist on wash day. The poster on the wall highlights some of the prices. Quarterly rental for the various types of cooker ranged from three shillings and sixpence (about 18p) to nine shillings (45p). The electric breakfast cooker was very similar to the 'Baby Belling' cooker we know today. The quarterly rental was two shillings and sixpence. Judging by the amount of fur being worn by the ladies in the picture this would have been quite a well-to-do gathering.

W.S..

Left: A busy shopping scene from the late 1930s. It shows Darley Street, looking down from the direction of Godwin Street. On the left of the picture, in the middle-distance, is the Savoy Cinema, owned by the ABC (Associated British Cinemas) a popular place of entertainment until 1939. Later, Marks and Spencer took over the site and extended their store here when the building was pulled down. It is likely that this picture was taken on a busy Saturday, judging by the number of shoppers in the picture. Note the fashions at the time, longer hemlines and every head covered with a hat of some description. Kirkgate Market can be seen on the right hand side of Darley Street. The market served Bradfordians very well up until 1973 when it was demolished and replaced by the Arndale Centre. On the left of the picture Barratt's shoe shop can be seen. The Northamptonshire-based shoe retailer had branches in almost every town in Britain.

Main picture: This wide panoramic view has been 'created' by joining two photographs in order to achieve this breathtaking result. The scene is known to date from 1946. Looking at it from the left, Kirkgate Market can be seen as it lies along Kirkgate. Shops which can be made out are, left to right, Stones, Willerby's, The Maypole Dairy Company, D. Wilson's bookshop, and Alexandre - the national chain of gents outfitters. Kino's Furriers shop was in Darley Street. Note the interesting two-wheeled device complete with chimney, in the bottom left hand quarter of the picture; it is actually a pitch-boiler, used by workmen to grout the sett paving. It is *not* a hot potato machine, though the modern reader could be forgiven for thinking that it was! The electric street light in the centre of the joined picture is mounted on a large D.C electric fuse box and it incorporates a very ornate traffic light. The street lamps on this pole were originally arc-lamps. On the other side of the road the slender street lamp was powered by high pressure gas.

The left hand side of Darley Street is dominated by another side of Kirkgate Market. The popular market reigned supreme between 1878 and 1973 and there was much consternation in Bradford when the decision to demolish it was announced. From left to right is Alexandres Gents tailors, then Kino's Furriers and Dr Scholls - which is now further up the street. Opposite we had Marks and Spencers- still to expand into the gap left by the demolition of the Savoy Cinema. Below was Woolworths - it would be strange not to have a 'Woollies' in a town or city the size of Bradford. Below this was Boots, and at the bottom Barclays Bank. This was always a very popular shopping area in Bradford, and the popularity was to reach even greater heights with the construction of the new shopping centre.

Above: Thornton Road as it enters Town Hall Square is featured in this busy 1950s scene. From left to right we see part of Taylor and Parsons Ironmongery and Furnishings ("Its wonderful what you can get at T & Ps"), Waldens Bedding Shop - formerly the (new) Tatler Cinema which closed after a fire in 1945. Wright and Peel (Leeford) Ltd., rainwear manufacturers in what had been a billiard hall, and, further down the block, Halfords cycle and car accessories shop. Across Tyrrel Street was Burtons, the well-known gents outfitters at the end of the block containing the Provincial Building Society.

"AT CHRISTMAS, PEOPLE WOULD QUEUE IN THEIR HUNDREDS TO BUY A PIE FROM PHILIP SMITH'S PORK BUTCHERS"

Below: A charming picture of Ivegate from Kirkgate dating from 1946. This most ancient of Bradford's streets is still much in the same form as seen here, although shop names have changed and the street has been pedestrianised with wall-to-wall stone flags.

Martins the Cleaners has gone, as has the barbers. Yates's Wine Lodge is still with us but the Old Crown has had a chequered career since 1946. Most people in Bradford would agree that the biggest loss to the street was Philip Smith's Pork butchers where queues would form, particularly at lunchtime, for their excellent pork and dripping sandwiches and marvellous meat pies. This was without doubt the best known small shop in Bradford and the owner won numerous prizes for the quality of his black puddings. Christmas time would see queues of over a hundred people waiting to buy a stand pie for the festivities - and this would often warrant a photograph depicting the scene in the 'Telegraph'.

The Grosvenor, a Melbourne house, has had many changes over the years, - a Berni Inn, the Ram's Revenge and now an Irish theme pub. The years after the end of the war would see many changes to the entertainment facilities available in Bradford. Eating out is taken for granted these days, but up until the 1950s the choice available to ordinary folk was limited to fish and chip take-aways, a handful of transport-style cafes, the restaurants inside the large department stores and an assortment of more refined tea rooms. The 1950s saw the arrival of Chinese restaurants and, later still the first Asian restaurants. Italian food didn't really attract a popular following until the 1970s, and it was later still that burger bars began to dominate the world of fast food take-aways.

W.S..

Above: This is the junction of Bridge Street and Market Street on a wet day in 1959. Following a closing-down sale the block of property formerly occupied by Timms and Dyson was soon to be demolished to make way for the construction of Ivebridge House and Telephone House, an early phase of the central area redevelopment. The building housing Barclays Bank has survived, though not as a bank. It started out as the Anglo-South American Bank before the Second World War. More mature readers may remember the Singer Sewing Machine shop which popular at this time, located just out of the picture to the left.

Below: John Street Open Market was built in 1931 on the site of Coppy Quarry. It was surrounded by John Street, Westgate and Rawson Road. On two sides stalls were covered by roofs, but by no means as closely as the present market. The crockery stall reminds one of the fellow who would sell you a tea service after having juggled with it and caught it all with a lot of clattering and drama. There was also a glass-cutter salesman whose speciality was cutting rings out of second-hand glass; very difficult indeed - and stringing them up in stalls across the stall. Ellis's Tools are still in business at Joseph Street, off Leeds Road.

Filaspun - 'A badge of success'

Filaspun Limited is a family firm, established in 1956 by Mr. R. Neil Smith, the present managing director, along with his late father and brother and also Mrs. Madge Roddis.

Holme Top Mills on Little Horton Lane was the original home of the company, running in tandem

with Mr. Neil Smith Senior who had a business weaving synthetic materials for dress goods, linings and tie cloths.

In 1982 Filaspun moved to their present site as Holme Top Mills were shortly to be demolished for a housing estate.

The company didn't move far, in fact just further up Little Horton Lane. This was the time when the workroom facilities were increased to enable tie making to be done on the premises to complement the university scarves already being manufactured.

The ties, badges and scarves were aimed at a specialised market of clubs, associations, universities and companies who required the production of their own unique crest or logo. The company is happy to supply small orders and large. Filaspun's designers are pleased to assist in helping to create a suitable design layout for each customer.

Since the early days, the company has diversified its product range as the market required. Many other textile items are now supplies - embroidered sweaters, sweatshirts, T-shirts, baseball hats, ladies scarves and headsquares - all with appropriate insignia for each customer. Their customer list includes many famous clubs and organisations, both at home and abroad.

Above: The staff of Filaspun in the 1980s.
Top left: The current Managing Director of Filaspun, Mr Neil Smith, pictured with his co-director, Carole Barr, both sporting the finished product.
Left: Filaspun's premises - Robert's Mill House in Little Horton Lane.

Man is made for co-operation

S o said Thomas Carlyle. The Co-operative Movement has played an important role in British social reform.

The First Fifty Years

In March 1860, in a cottage at Wood Road, West Bowling, a group of mill operatives met, intent on forming a Co-operative Society. Each member saved sixpence a week and a shop was opened at the top of Adelaide Street. The society was registered as 'Bradford Provident Society' and by the end of the year there were 201 members, sales amounted to £795 and profits were £33 2s 5d.

Another group of workers set up the 'Bradford Industrial Society which opened its first shop at 30, Queensgate in December of the same year. It had 130 members and Share Capital amounted to £150. Eight years later, these two groups amalgamated to form the Bradford Provident Industrial Society Ltd.

Confidence in the power of Co-operation steadily grew. By 1870, capital had reached £13,117 whilst annual sales were £53,469 which realised a bonus of a shilling in the pound. A fortunate speculation in buying land at Heaton Road enabled the society to develop its policy of house building for its members. An ambitious programme was set up which included the businesses of manufactures, farmers, millers and wholesale dealers.

A large influx of members and capital made possible the purchase of a central site at Sunbridge Road. Premises containing departments and offices were opened in 1895. These served for 40 years before they were demolished to make way for a more modern 'Emporium'

We beg to announce that within a **very short time** a new section will be opened to cater for this business. Patrons will find that the section has been very well appointed and that the assistants are properly trained to undertake all branches of ladies' hairdressing. Well known "perming" systems will be essentially reasonable. Beauty problems will also be dealt with and the products of manufacturers of repute will be available for salon use and for sale. ¶ Club coupons will be accepted, of course, as well as cash. ¶ Announcements of the opening date will appear within the next week or two. May we respectfully suggest that you reserve your appointments for your own society?

Ladies' Hairdressing

By 1900 the work of several Co-operative Societies was overlapping, but only two of them were willing to amalgamate. These two, therefore, the Bowling Old Lane and the Bradford Provident Industrial became, in 1901, the City of Bradford Co-operative Society Ltd. The total membership was now 20,206 and further saving was encouraged by a dividend of 3s in the pound.

In 1910 the Drapery Department had spilled over from Sunbridge Road and premises were rented for it in Market Street. The Jubilee of the society was fittingly celebrated, with exhibitions and demonstrations. A history of its 50 years was prepared and distributed, mentioning the Coal Department which had begun dealing in 1880, the stables and Traffic, Laundry, Bakery, Grocery & Butchery, Footwear, Tailoring, Dispensing and Furnishing.

By now the Society employed 800 and dividends of £1,500,000 had been paid. It had built 200 houses for

its members to rent and opened a mortgage department.

The Great War

In 1911, the year the National Congress visited Bradford, the Collective Life Assurance was a further amenity offered to members, with painting and decorating following three years later. After that the war took its toll in wealth and lives and altered the outlook of Co-operators in regard to national affairs. Government officials visited the society and took clothing and horses for the army. National service removed the bulk of the workforce. Despite profiteering and campaigns of price-raising, the 'Co-op' returned the fullest possible advantages for its members.

Public confidence in the Society's policy led to a huge increase in membership which remained even when rationing regularised things to a large degree. Later, however, the increased membership was ignored when the Society's rations were being estimated and there was dissatisfaction when loyally registered members' supplies proved insufficient. The government intervened and redressed members' grievances and the movement began to realise its power.

The New Emporium Scheme

In 1919 a reorganisation scheme was launched and for the first time sales exceeded a million pounds. On the other hand, changed money values and rapidly falling prices brought the dividend down to 9d, with consequent loss of members.

Between 1925 and 1933, four more societies, the Eccleshill Industrial, the Greengates, Allerton Industrial and Birkenshaw amalgamated with the City of Bradford group, bringing total membership to over 37,000 and vastly increasing the financial stability of the society. A Summer Holiday Savings Club was begun and, in 1928 the Society adopted a superannuation scheme for its 1,200 employees.

Above: The Bridge Street premises. **Left:** *A letterhead dating from the 1950s.* **Top right:** *The Co-op at Wibsey.* **Centre left:** *The cottage where it all began!* **Facing page, top left:** *The Co-op old premises on Sunbridge Road.* **Facing page, centre left:** *A 1960s advertisement which more or less speaks for itself!* **Facing page, bottom right:** *The Drapery department in the 1960s.*

were made to it until rules came into force granting a half, and later one whole per cent of the Society's net profit to the Committee's discretion. The activities it organised were many, varied and imaginative. For the children there were carnivals, junior guilds and lantern lectures. Adolescents had Comrades' Circles, technical training classes were set up for employees, concerts and social evenings were arranged and the Aged Members' Treats were much appreciated.

The Educational Institute in Oddfellows Court accommodated the Department

The 'Emporium Scheme' was to cost approximately £145,000. The first portion was completed and declared open in September 1934. Sales that year reached £1,289,504 and it was felt to be the beginning of better times. However, a continued slump in the city's industry caused much unemployment and soon there was anxiety about trade turnover in the new building. An appeal was made to bring membership up to 40,000.

Here They Are!

The NEW Winter Coats

The best in Fashion Fabric and Tailoring at their price.

★

Flattering New Shades

★

In Misses, Women's and Large Sizes.

★

There's one here for you at a price you have in mind.

COATS *with Variation*

Come and see for yourself

Fashion Showroom - First Floor
EMPORIUM - SUNBRIDGE ROAD

The Men's Guild formed by the committee in 1909 predated the National Men's Guild Movement. At weekly meetings through the winter, Co-operative topics were ventilated and discussed.

In February 1936 a propaganda campaign aimed to increase membership from 38,000 to 40,000. A new coupon scheme was due to be introduced after the half year. It had to be delayed for a while because increased taxation on tea meant reprinting the labels. Twice a year coupons could be exchanged for cash. In the same year a plan was launched to recognise all members' Golden Wedding anniversaries with a letter of congratulation and a cake.

In 1939 President Mr. W. Hirst retired after 25 years' devoted service. In the Emporium, 'refuge rooms'

The Emporium's second portion was opened in February 1936. The new store soon became known and appreciated as the finest place to shop in the north of England.

Activities of the Education Committee
The committee was formed in 1900. Money grants

were prepared in the basements in case of air raids, some of them gas-proofed.

Christmas 1940 saw the last edition of the magazine because of paper shortage. In that year, under the auspices of the Lord Mayor's Services Comforts Fund, the Society's Grocery Department received an order to pack 3,000 parcels as gifts for the Bradford men in the armed forces. They contained 1lb fruit cake, a tin of Oxo cubes a quarter pound each of chocolate and other sweets, a tablet of soap, 25 cigarettes, a tin of boot polish and a tube of toothpaste. Christmas 1940 saw the last edition of the Co-op magazine for a while owing to the wartime scarcity of

Society which resulted in agreement to combine with the City of Bradford branch. Arising from this example, a merger was proposed that also included Buttershaw & Wibsey, Clayton, Great Horton, Queensbury, Thornton and Wilsden. Great Horton, Queensbury and Thornton were rejected but the rest were incorporated into the Bradford & District Co-operative Society in 1960.

Cut prices at the supermarket have taken the place of saving through dividends in the intervening forty years but the 'Co-op' has followed the self-service trend and there are very few town or city centres where the Society is not represented on the high street.

*Above: The Co-op at Heaton Syke. **Left:** The Queensbury Industrial Society which is now the site of the Co-op Food Fair supermarket. **Facing page, top:** The dispensing department from the 1960s. **Facing page, centre:** Winter coats for fashion conscious sixties women. **Facing page, bottom:** The Co-op on Manchester Road. **Below:** The Sunbridge Road Emporium (now known as Sunwin House) from the outside, after extensive renovations in the 1960s.*

paper. Unfortunately, the workers lost their friendly supply of company news and researchers lost a wonderful account of the everyday -or at least every month- affairs of the various institutions under the umbrella of the Society.

In 1955, the Education Department held an adult class on 'The Co-operative Society as an employer.' Surprisingly, the take up was disappointing. There was a great enthusiasm however for the dressmaking lessons which ended with a display of the garments made. The Bradford Group's Choral Society competed in the annual north east Choral Festival.

By 1956 membership stood at 40,774 and share capital at £738,642, disappointingly a decrease of more than £4,000 on the previous year.

In November 1959, discussions were held with the Denholme Industrial Co-operative

Everything for everyone under one roof!

The very beginnings of Kirkgate Market go back to 1251 when King Henry III granted to Edmund de Lacy, "that he and his heirs for ever shall have one market every week at his manor of Brafford."

In 1866 the Corporation leased the market rights from Benjamin's descendant, Miss Elizabeth Rawson for 999 years at £5,000 a year. They demolished the Manor Hall to make way for the construction of a covered market. This was built in two stages and finished in May 1878 at a cost of £83,381.

During the 1930s there was considerable debate about the future of the market. There was a proposition that it should be demolished and moved elsewhere, but public opposition to this plan meant that nothing was done. The arguments rumbled on until, by 1973, the deed was almost complete. The Kirkgate Market Action Committee continued to press for refurbishment rather than destruction. In 1974 photographs were printed in the Telegraph & Argus showing the demolished site.

At first it was run under the auspices of the church, with the old Market Cross now in the 'Westgate Box' to prove it. A Benjamin Rawson, who acquired the market rights in the 18th century, moved it from Westgate to Market House, Bank Street and this move marked the end of the church's influence.

By 1824, this site too was proving to be too small and there was a further move to Manor Hall in Kirkgate which is where the story really starts for Kirkgate Market. When stalls were first set up around the once-fine Manor Hall, there were some objections and reference made to 'a beggarly array of stalls and shambles.' The objectors met with little success and the Kirkgate Market, originally called the Butter Market, has remained on this site ever since.

By 1976 both phases of the new Kirkgate Arndale Centre were complete and its backers had persuaded the public that it was 'a valuable asset to the city's commercial life.' Shopping malls were added to make a complete shopping centre which then remained unaltered for almost 14 years.

In 1988, refurbishment was deemed necessary and this work continued for almost twelve months, during which the centre remained open every single day. When the changes, which had cost over three and a half million pounds, were complete, the site was renamed the Kirkgate Shopping Centre. The integral site is bounded by Kirkgate, Westgate, Darley Street and Godwin Street.

The car park and the Kirkgate Market are part of the building but they belong to the Bradford Council. The rest of the centre belongs to Prudential Assurance Company Ltd. Early in 1987 Prudential Property Management had offered to undertake the refurbishment and produced their plans.

The centre's tenants were consulted at all stages and their views taken into account. Each week a newsletter was sent to all units to keep them abreast of the work in progress. Four Kirkgate Reviews were published to keep the public informed.

New retail units called Gazebos were introduced to bring in smaller, individual retailers, as well as a Kiddie Ride carousel. An Information Bureau was added, staffed with the management's personnel and the female staff were issued with smart new uniforms of blazers and slacks in keeping with the new image. The Kirkgate Shopping Centre has the second biggest car park in the city centre which is available for general use, not just for those who patronise the centre.

In 1997 the centre is having its two main entrances redecorated and brought up to date and a new logo will be introduced. The centre is currently fully let with the ultimate in choice for shoppers.

Above: A lively café which serves delicious food to the weary shopper. *Facing page, top left:* Completed in May 1878, the Kirkgate Market has always been a popular spot for Bradfordians who just can't resist a bargain! *Facing page, bottom right:* The information desk is staffed by people who can help with all sorts of information. *Left:* A plaque which stands inside the shopping centre. *Below:* An artist's impression of how the Arcade will look after the renovations due to begin in 1997.

A market heritage spanning seven centuries

The first market charter in Bradford was granted to Edmund de Lacy by King Henry III in April 1251. It was first held in the vicinity of the Parish Church (now the Cathedral). At that time the population of Bradford was in the region of 650 persons and the principal articles of food were oatmeal porridge, and bread. Vegetables were imported from Holland and only the rich could afford them.

Later, the market was moved to the bottom of Westgate, which remained the centre until 1801. The Market Place in Westgate was the triangular opening at the top of Kirkgate and Ivegate. Two sides of the opening were occupied by butchers' shambles, having slaughterhouses in the immediate neighbourhood. An ancient market cross stood not far from the top of Ivegate. During the Civil Wars, the top of the cross was said to have been broken off by the over-zealous Puritans in a desire to obliterate all traces of the established church which they so stoutly condemned.

The toll booth was in Ivegate, the upper portion of it being the 'Hall of Pleas' comprised in the grant of the Manor by King Charles 1. Underneath was the town's dungeon, which was said to have been divided into two compartments, one for male and the other for female delinquents. The lower part of the cross can still be seen in the Westgate entrance to Kirkgate Market In 1795 the market rights were purchased by the Rawson family.

In 1801 they moved operations to New Street, renamed, for obvious reasons, Market Street. The new market hall built there was condemned by the people of Bradford for its 'foreign' appearance and no objections were voiced when it was pulled down.

It served as a market until 1824 and was afterwards used as a piece market when the old Piece Hall in Kirkgate became too congested.

In 1824, the Lord of the Manor built a market house, later known as the Butter Market. In addition to the Market House there were areas used as open markets with canvas covered stalls.

Soon, the Corporation became concerned about conditions in the town centre. Cattle fairs, horse fairs, the abattoir and similar activities were impeding ordinary traffic and endangering public safety. The Town Council in 1865 considered purchasing the manorial rights of Bradford from the Lady of the Manor, Miss Elizabeth Rawson.

In September, a motion was proposed by Alderman Farrar that the council should apply to the government for a 99 year lease on the property around the market place, Kirkgate, and the Fair Ground, Darley Street. The right to hold markets and fairs within the borough were purchased for £5,000 a year during the term of the lease.

Above: A delightful 1950s picture of an indoor market stall when Bradford Markets were celebrating seven hundred years in existence. Left: Where it all began.....the Manor Hall and old Market Place. Facing page: The Rawson Place Market was subject to an air raid on 31st August 1940. The whole of the left side of the building was destroyed, taking with it 21 fruiterers, five provision and six meat stalls in the interior along with seven exterior shops in Rawson Place, John Street and James Street. The market was closed and didn't re-open until 1957. Below: Rawson Place Market, dating from the War years, before it was bombed in a night time air raid.

Continued overleaf

Eighty three years later, in 1949, after failed attempts in 1909 and 1922, negotiations were begun for the Corporation to purchase outright these Market Rights and leasehold property. They were completed in March 1951 at a price of £163,800.

The owner of market rights is entitled to establish markets and protect them from rival operations

Now the Corporation was authorised to alter or remove markets and fairs to more suitable localities, to lease premises for cattle markets, if necessary putting up suitable buildings. They could levy and receive tolls if they agreed to traders other than their own using the rights they had purchased. The act which sanctioned these arrangements received royal assent in July 1866.

being set up within a distance of six and two thirds miles. Rival markets are prevented from operating by the owner obtaining a High Court injunction.

The rights are therefore considered to be very valuable. Market rights are still referred to and used today, for example in the licensing of car boot sales which are deemed to be markets.

Markets are part of Bradford's history and tradition. After 1866, major investment took place in the markets. For example, three new markets were built, Kirkgate Market, Rawson Market and St. James' Wholesale Market.

The investment goes on today with the Rawson Market Redevelopment Scheme costing £6 million, plus the provision of a Temporary Market, costing £1 million to accommodate stall-holders whilst the Redevelopment takes place.

The markets are very profitable for the Council, having contributed £12

million over the last ten years to the Council's General Fund for the benefit of local taxpayers.

Above : A devastating fire swept through John Street Market on 5th November 1977, razing it to the ground in just a matter of hours. It has since been rebuilt and remains one of Bradford's most popular venues for a bargain. *Top:* The interior of Kirkgate Market during the early 1950s. *Facing page, top left:* John Street Market from John's Court in the 1940s. *Facing page top right:* John Street Market from around the same time. *Facing page, bottom:* A wonderful array of goods have always been available at John Street and the market has always teemed with eager bargain hunters.

Wheels of time

Right: An excellent insight into the Central Area Redevelopment Scheme in progress, viewed from the Midland Hotel towards the Exchange Station. Gerrards were the contractors for the building works for the Hammerson Group of Companies, and the Architects were Clyde Young and Bernard Engle. Gerrards site huts contrast with the City Engineers modest accommodation behind, engaged in extending Cheapside across Market Street and Broadway to the new Forster Square. A new building, Forster House, was to occupy the space between Kirkgate and Cheapside; Kirkgate was to become Station Forecourt.

The trolley buses were to stop running on the Cross Flatts route in 1963, a portent of things to come, thus this picture is likely to date from about 1962. The new buildings in the picture make good use of Portland Stone facings, and contrasting dark marble. The BDA building of 1867 became Pennine House - council offices with underground car park built between Well Street (the old route to Leeds Rd) and the new Petergate. Some shops were already open in the Central House block, but not British Home Stores. The roof became a car park.

Below: The early 1960s, and the area at the bottom of Manchester Road is recorded in this scene. This was an increasingly busy part of Bradford, in terms of road traffic at least. The visibility of the point-duty policeman must have been an issue, judging by the lengths that had been gone to in order to make it easier for the passing cars to see him; white gloves, a crude but brightly painted platform and the white waterproof coat all combine to make the 'bobby' stand out. At one time a white helmet cover was used by police officers to make them even more noticeable.

Behind the 'bobby' is the building housing the Yorkshire Penny Bank, and further along the road the Odeon and Oddfellow's Arms can be seen on the left. Most of the buildings in the view were pulled down at the dawn of the 1970s.

Left: A busy scene showing Forster Square and believed to date from between 1945 and 1949. The various methods of transport in the picture are interesting and help us to estimate the date of the photograph. The trams on the right of the scene look very old fashioned in comparison to the two trolley buses on the left. It is known that trams ceased running on the Bradford Moor route (No. 30) in 1949. It is obvious that the picture was not taken during wartime; had it been, the lights of the various vehicles in the scene would have been masked as part of the air-raid precautions, and, of course, the passers-by would have been required to have their gas-masks with them. The trolley buses had loaded their passengers from a covered platform since 1939, and did so until 1949 when the overhead wires were reorganised. After 1949 passengers boarded from the footway to the right of the photograph. The trolley bus on the left is about to depart for Frizinghall.

Above: This is the Jowett Javelin assembly line at the Idle Works between 1947 and 1954, during which time 22,700 motors were built here. It was a 1500cc 80 MPH, six-seater car which won the Monte Carlo Rally in 1949. Remarkably the plucky vehicle managed an average speed of more than 65 MPH over a distance of 1700 miles. A sports model, the Jupiter, was also built here, 830 units being produced in all.

Motor bodies were supplied by Briggs Motor Bodies of Doncaster. When Jowett's ran up against hard times and Briggs were bought out by Fords in 1953, Calcott Reilly sold out to the International Harvester Co. who then manufactured agricultural tractors at Idle.

Jowett Motors was established in 1906 by William and Ben Jowett who made their first 'light' car - a 2 seater, 7 horse-power, flat-twin, weighing just 6cwt. Their slogan was 'the little engine with the big pull.' Bradford vans and pick-ups were also built here. Jowett Engineering manufactured spare parts until 1964. The site of the old car factory is now Morrisons Enterprise 5 shopping and light industrial complex.

Right: Engine testing 1950s style. A twin cylinder horizontally-opposed engine is being put through its paces on the test bench. It was engines like this which powered the Jowett Bradford Van, by far the most successful vehicle produced at the Idle plant. For many years the flat twin produced just 7 horse power (hp) but development increased this to 9 hp

in 1935. Pre-war advertising claims described how "the engine provides balanced-power for the roomiest light-car ever built." It went on.. "the appetite of a canary, the strength of a lion and the docility of a lamb...."

Right: An interior scene at the Idle works showing the degreasing plant in operation. This process was essential in order to make the surface of the components clean enough to paint. Some of the castings in the photograph look as if they may have been intended for gearbox assembly. Jowett's had an unhappy experience when they tried to design and build their own gearboxes. The outcome was that ratios could not be selected properly, or the cars stuck in gear.... even before they had left the factory. During the crisis, for that is what the situation became, vehicles were parked all over the plant and rented fields beyond, awaiting repairs and modifications to the ill-fated gearboxes.

Below: Without doubt, the Bradford Van was the unsung hero of the Jowett company. It sold in greater numbers than any of the other models produced at the Idle works - nearly twice as many Bradford's than Javelins were built for example, and nearly 50 vans were sold for every one Jupiter sports car! The Bradford was Jowett's first post-war offering but it still relied upon the old flat twin engine for its motive power. Business people loved them for

their reliability and durability, but most of all they loved the low petrol consumption and pulling power which was reputed to 'negotiate any load on any road.' The two cylinder engine developed 9 horse power (about as much as a small motorbike in modern times) but had exceptional levels of torque which won it many friends in motoring circles. The Bradford van was the only product which really made money for the firm; it was used to develop the other vehicles in the range, especially the Jupiter, but it was not enough to guarantee the future success of car production in Bradford.

Right: "This way up" says the manager in the trilby hat, as the security guard carefully checks the paperwork with the driver, to ensure that precisely *one* tractor is accounted for on the despatch note. In truth, we are unsure why the departure of this solitary machine warranted a formal photograph. Perhaps it was the first tractor to leave the plant... or the first of many to be exported overseas? Whatever the reason, it provides a nostalgic look backwards at the world of work.

PRIDE IN FACTORY
FOUNDATION — A QUALITY
LAID — PRODUCT
BRADFORD MADE

Left: During the years after International Harvesters began manufacturing agricultural tractors at the former Jowett Factory they appeared conscious of the need to demonstrate their success to the workforce and the rest of Bradford as a whole. The reference to 'pride' in this photograph seems ahead of its time. It is much more akin to the Japanese-style management techniques we hear of in modern times than the calamitous relationships in the motor industry which blighted the 1960s and 1970s, allowing foreign competitors to gain a foothold in domestic markets which would later ruin many motor manufacturers. The men and women of Bradford's tractor factory sent machines to markets all over the world, despite stiff competition from other manufacturers at home and abroad.

Below left: The 25,000th 'B250' model is ready for delivery, resplendent in her distinctive red livery, and seen here with the General Manager of the idle works at the wheel. Piles of chunky tyres higher than a man can be seen in the background of the photograph (close your eyes and you can smell the deep, rich aroma of the rubber) and other machines queue up for pre-delivery testing prior to shipping all over the world. This photograph is at least 40 years old, yet many of these machines are still in working order on the farms and small holdings in scores of different countries around the globe. Well done Bradford!

Below centre: A carefully arranged picture taken to mark the production of the 100,000th International Harvester Tractor produced at the Idle works. International Harvester took over the Jowett company in 1954. There is something significant about the photograph; producing tractors was obviously *men's business* in the 1950s... not a woman in sight in this picture! Note too that a brown or white overall was virtually obligatory in the tractor trade.

Below right: Here we see the tractor assembly line in the same works following acquisition by the International Harvester Company. The work appears to be very labour intensive and is organised along traditional car assembly line principles, despite the heavier weight of the machines involved. There is something almost symbolic in the composition of this photograph; two men busy working on the vehicle standing on the shop-floor, with one man in a pit underneath the tractor fitting another component at the rear. The conditions will seem rather basic to people used to modern working environments; this was a sad feature of many British engineering concerns in the '50s and '60s. The symbolism is reinforced by the presence of the supervisor in the background in his long, grey overall.

A E Goetze. A proud history - an even brighter future

When Elijah Hepworth first established his general engineering and repair company, 'E Hepworth & Sons' in 1907, the world was a very different place from today. Edward VII was on the throne, Sir Henry Campbell-Bannerman was prime minister, Britain ruled an empire and only a few of the very richest people in society owned a car. The firm at Aldermanbury in those days was mainly involved with general engineering and repair work but the manufacture of piston rings soon followed. The first order recorded was for a number of pins for woodworking machinery.

When, in 1910 the company became Hepworth and Grandage, its activities widened to include the manufacture of cast iron pistons. In 1913 business had improved so as to need the larger premises in Manchester Road. By the time Elijah Hepworth senior retired in 1916, another move was required, this time to the Wakefield Road site which formerly belonged to Bowling Ironworks. Here, the company employed a hundred men who, in 1920 began to make the first aluminium alloy pistons. A few years later, gudgeon pins and cylinder liners were added to the product line.

In 1926 the first replacement parts catalogues were issued and the name Hepolite was coined. This was the year of the company's first successes in the world of motorsport.

In 1928, Hepworth and Grandage became a public limited company. During 1938 the first engine test bed was installed. The company now runs seventeen of them for the development of new pistons.

All the following pictures are taken from a 1930s photograph album.

Above: The machine shop. Centre left: Casting liners. Below left: Machining pistons. Below: The Chemical Laboratory.

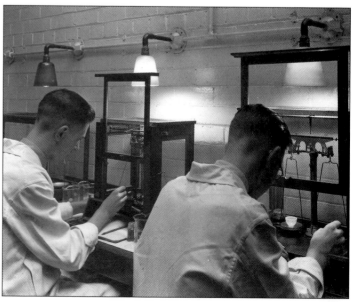

The importance of the company in the 40s is testified to by a visit from Winston Churchill, accompanied by Archibald Sinclair and Ernest Bevan in 1942. This was followed in 1944 by a visit from Mary, the Princess Royal.

The Second World War increased the work force from 1,400 in 1939 to 4,000 by 1945. This dropped back to 3,000 with the return of peace. In 1947, the company AE Holdings was formed, by the amalgamation of Brico, Hepworth and Grandage and Wellworthy. H&G introduced its famous W-Design pistons in the following year. In 1950 the Saltaire factory was bought from Alfred Scott, the creator of the well-known Scott Motor cycles. Saltaire manufactured pistons up to 1982 when production was transferred back to Bradford.

The fifties brought a list of moves forward. The Yeadon factory was purchased from Arrow Aircraft and began the production of turbine blades. Work began on levelling 'Dross Hill' to make way for a new warehouse, now Piston Manufacturing Facility and the office block which was opened in 1957 by Stirling Moss who, only weeks later won the British Grand Prix at Aintree.

1957 was the company's Golden Jubilee year. Celebrations included the famous trip to Blackpool by all 3,500 employees. In 1959, Hepolite products achieved successes with Aston Martin at Le Mans and with Stirling Moss and Jack Brabham (World Champion) in Formula 1. Highlights of the sixties were the opening of new labs, and a visit from Willie Whitelaw. Graham Hill, who became World Champion, drove the Lotus Ford 49 which used Hepolite piston assemblies.

In 1977, Mr. Jack Hepworth, 'King Hep' retired, leaving the company without a Hepworth at the helm for the first time in its history. Awards since then have included the Queen's Award for Export in 1987 and the Rover Bronze award ten years later. In 1988, with the support of many Bradford personnel, piston production was established at South Bend, USA. In 1994 the company became known as AE Goetze after its parent company T&N purchased the German piston ring giant, Goetze AG.

In 90 years, Elijah's company has grown from a small family business in Bradford to become part of this major international concern.

Top right: This programme was issued for the Golden Jubilee of the company in 1957.
Top left: The trip to Blackpool by all 4,000 employees in 1957 to celebrate the Jubilee.

Rossefield Motor Co Ltd. A national centre for three-wheeled motoring

In 1946, no longer needed to fight for his country, Jack Calthorpe began attending military auctions to bid for ex-army motorcycles, which were now, like himself, surplus to the government's requirements. Ready to use whatever was to hand in order to establish himself in business, his first premises were a converted guard's van on a railway siding in Canal Road. Soon he was able to afford better things.

On rented British Rail land he put up a garage that served him until his company moved to Manningham Lane in the 1950s.
Here, under the name F&C (Mobyke Spares), they occupied two shops opposite one another and sold bubble cars and the now legendary motor cycles of the period, Panther, BSA, DOT, and Ariel.

The business became part of the area's life, so that, when the building was destroyed by fire in 1994,

John Calthorpe could say, 'Amazing the number of people who have phoned me to mourn the passing of our old shop -especially since we have not been there for 25 years.'

To everyone's astonishment, whilst at this address the firm took on the agency for the unheard-of Lambretta scooter, which, a few years later, took the country by storm. They stayed with Lambrettas until they ceased to be made in the seventies.

Because the law required only a motor cycle licence for the driving of a Reliant car, F&C started selling Reliants in the sixties. In 1972 the company moved from Manningham Lane to its present site in Emm Lane, Heaton. At the same time the name was changed from Mobyke Spares to Rossefield Motor Company Ltd.

Starting as a small village petrol station, the site has been developed into a spacious modern complex with a 12 car showroom, a workshop and bodyshop and a forecourt displaying approximately thirty used Reliants.

John Calthorpe officially joined the company when he reached the age of 16 in 1972, although he had worked in the garage at weekends and in school holidays for as long as he can remember. He worked alongside his father's co-directors until they retired in 1992 since when he has had sole control of the business.

Rossefield is now one of the largest stockists and dealers in Reliants in the UK. They regularly sell and deliver cars to all parts of Scotland and make frequent trips to Belfast. A quarter of all spare parts are sold through the firm's postal service. Four members of staff have over a century of Reliant experience between them.

Above: The company began to sell Reliants in the 1960s due to the regulations governing driving restrictions. It was possible to drive a Reliant without a full licence which meant that it was highly popular with those who were a little scared of exams!

Top: A Lambretta, a highly popular scooter which ended its reign in the 1970s. It ran on 2 stroke fuel and was capable of 80 miles to the gallon.

Above left: An Isetta Bubblecar dating from the 1950s on display at a motor show.

Left: The inside of the shop was an Aladdin's cave for the initiated. The wonderful smell of oil pervaded and this was irrisistable to most motor enthusiasts.Facing page, top right: The shop on Manningham Lane that everyone remembers. The company occupied these premises in the 1950s until 1972 when they moved to Heaton.

Facing page, bottom left: Mr Calthorpe in a Messerschmidt, dating from the 1950s.

Facing page, top left: An early advertisement. A far cry from the Reliant on the roads today.

The fascinating story of Waddingtons

Eighteen-eighty-seven was an eventful year. In it, Queen Victoria celebrated her Golden Jubilee, Sir Arthur Conan-Doyle published his first detective story, 'A Study in Scarlet', and Field Marshal Viscount Montgomery was born. In addition, it was the year when a butcher named Priestley Waddington and a stone quarrier called Richard Jarratt together formed a company that produced dripping, glue, bone meal and fertilisers.

Their premises are believed to have been Crossley Hall Works on Jessey Street in Fairweather Green, Bradford. There, using basic boiling pans, they processed waste material from butchers' shops and abattoirs.

Raw materials

Today, the company's equipment includes fully automatic continuous cookers, presses and grinders but their raw materials are just the same.

With a horse-drawn carriage, they delivered dripping in open buckets with just a piece of paper on top as a nod in the direction of hygiene. Business went less well than they had hoped and eventually Priestley's brother, Sam Waddington, of J. Waddington in Keighley, had to rescue them financially at the cost of letting him take the firm over. No-one had a particular job. Each of the three did what was most urgent at any given moment!

Top left: Priestley Waddington, the butcher from Fairweather Green who went into partnership with (strangely enough) a quarrier, Richard Jarrett.
Below: Abe Waddington, second generation of the family, more famous perhaps for his abilities on the cricket fields.

Second generation

The company remained in these premises for 80 years. During that time the first generation of Waddingtons gave place to the second in the persons of Sam, Peter and not least Abe, who is better remembered for his prowess in the Yorkshire County Cricket team between 1919 and 1926. In 1921/2 he was amongst the English players who toured Australia.

The Second World War necessitated a break in the company's

Left: Richard Jarrett. It isn't known why a quarrier would want to establish a dripping, bone meal and fertiliser company but he did! **Below left and below:** *Sam Waddington II, second generation of the family to run the business.*

usual business. Its office was taken over by the Ministry of supply and, under the title 'Fabons Limited' it controlled from Fairweather Green the supply of palm kernel oil to the north east.

Stockbridge

After the war the company returned to its usual production of tallow, dripping, bone meal and meat for pet foods. Another member of the family, John Waddington, who owned Stockbridge works at Stockbridge, Keighley, came to join them in 1945.
In time, the business passed to Keith Waddington, who, in 1967, had to move his premises.

Failing to grant the planning permission he sought, Bradford City Council instead moved his company to the Refinery in Filey Street. By this time, commerce and industry were vastly changed, so that the firm's customers are now soap manufacturers, the chemical industries and fish and chip shops.

The Waddingtons currently running the business are Messrs Mark and Nicholas who have a staff of forty. They have had their problems. They would be the first to agree that, though useful, even necessary, theirs is not a sweetly scented business.

They claim and believe however that they

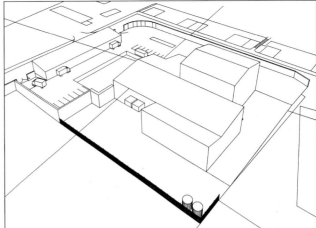

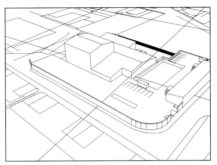

living employee who for 50 years drove a Bedford lorry for them, collecting bones and animal waste. Tommy turned up without fail in snow, hail and shine, to do his round with cheerfulness and good nature. 'They are the best people you could work for,' he says.

Tommy has good reasons for his opinion, as one of the company secretaries visits weekly having collected his pension. (This says all that needs to be said about the way the company looks after its employees, past and present!)

Tommy still gets his Christmas box from Waddingtons' who are hoping very much that their old employee will be fit enough to open their new factory next year.

have been blamed for problems which should rightfully lie at the door of the managers of Bradford Beck and the sanitary inspectors responsible for Bradford drains.

These problems, together with all the fears concerning BSE and CJD have made life difficult. The Waddingtons have a positive attitude and intend to win back their markets and improve, continually their manufacturing base and their environmental awareness. In 1998 they will be moving into a new, purpose-built factory in Buck Street.

Let Mr. Tommy Owen have the last word. Now aged 91, he is Waddingtons' oldest

Above: The firm are soon to move to a new purpose-built factory at Buck Street. The computer generated plans show a perspective of the factory from the North West (top) and South East (lower picture).

Left: Long before the internal combustion engine made its impact a more sedate form of local transportation was used for local deliveries. The cart is loaded with buckets of dripping for delivery with only a thin cloth separating the dripping from the hungry insects! The picture dates from the turn of the century, when Waddingtons would have been established around twenty years and were still based at Fairweather Green.

A story of progress and proud heritage

In the beginning

Early in 1920, Sydney Packett gave £20 for the key of a small room on the 3rd floor of No. 1, Ivegate, Bradford. However, the firm next door, which sold ladies' blouses, had the lock removed and a new one fitted while Mr. Packett was out. Thus, he had to go to law before he could set up, on his 33rd birthday, his business as an insurance broker.

So soon after the Great War, there was no chance of a separate telephone. Fortunately, the architect on the floor below, a Mr. Atkinson, kindly agreed to let him have a joint line. The brass plate at the street door read, ' Incorporated Insurance Broker & Adviser.'

At first Mr. Packett's most pressing concern was cash. The manager of Martin's Bank in Tyrrel Street asked for securities for deposit against a possible loan but Mr. Packett had none. However he mentioned that Colonel Morris of Halifax, a director of the bank, would speak for him. The colonel recommended that Mr. Packett should be advanced whatever sum he required and proved helpful in many other ways. Business went well and the overdraft was soon paid off.

Another early difficulty was Mr. Packett's need to seek business during the day to work on at night. This meant that that the office was left empty. Mrs. Packett was helpful, manning the office when she could, but full time assistance was obviously needed. Mr. Packett was glad to secure the services of a young clerk, Kenneth Fox. Unfortunately for both himself and his employer, Mr. Fox was away from work for four months with pneumonia during his first year.

'YOU SECURE YOUR POLICIES DO THEY SECURE YOU?'

Sydney Packett & Sons Ltd.

for all classes of

INSURANCE

FIRE
LIFE
MARINE
ACCIDENT
STAFF PENSIONS
ENGINEERING &c.

INCORPORATED INSURANCE BROKERS
LLOYDS BANK CHAMBERS
HUSTLERGATE
BRADFORD
YORKS.

Telephone No
BFD. 27397

Telegrams:-
"PACKETT"
BRADFORD

He returned, however, to give many years' loyal service and eventually to become a director. Before long an arrangement was made with J. W. Ackroyd & Son, jointly to do commercial and private house inventories and valuations and to undertake fire loss settlements. This was very hard work, sometimes until the early hours of the morning, but the fees made Mr. Packett a modest living and built up the insurance side of the business. Soon he was able to visit his clients in a car with a chauffeur, which was fortunate as he did not hold a driving licence.

In 1927, with several other gentlemen prominent on the insurance scene, he formed the Insurance Advisory Section of Bradford Chamber of Commerce. For many years he was a member of the committee and he served a term as Chairman.

In 1928 a move was made to more spacious premises in Lloyds Bank Chambers, Hustlergate, Bradford, from where the firm still operates, though now it has spread to three floors of the building.

The next decade
In the 1930s competition for business was very keen, and the West Riding of Yorkshire in particular was becoming broker conscious. Older firms were expanding and new ones starting up and it would hardly be an exaggeration to say there were more insurance brokers in Bradford compared with the population than any other city in the country.

Mr. Packett had been a member of Bradford Wool Exchange for some time. The Exchange thronged with the chiefs and representatives of the textile and associated industries and insurance men abounded as members. Soon Mr. Packett was appointed to act as

broker and adviser to one of the largest textile groups in the country.

During the thirties, apart from his insurance interests, Mr. Packett undertook much public work. As a city councillor, he served on the Baths Committee and the Conditioning House, Transport and Watch Committees.

Continued overleaf

Above: *Hustlergate, Bradford, home of Sydney Packett & Sons Ltd since 1928. Lloyds Bank Chambers are just above the centre of the photograph with the old Swan Arcade just below. Knocked down in the 1960s, the Swan Arcade was a sad loss to the city.* **Facing page, top right:** *A brochure dating from 1980s which shows the company's premises on Hustlergate.* **Facing page, bottom left:** *Mr Sydney Packett, founder of the company, in a photograph dating from the mid 1930s.*

He did voluntary work in the administration of Public Assistance, as well as being President of the Insurance Institute of Bradford (1930-31) and a long-serving member of the Yorkshire and North Eastern District Committee of the Corporation of Insurance Brokers. He took an interest in Bradford City Boys' Club, founding and serving on the committee that ran it. In 1939, at the outbreak of the Second World War, Mr. Packett formed the Wool Insurance Committee with two other brokers, to advise the industry and to deal with the handling of Marine Insurance for the Wool Control.

During the War

The detrimental effects of war in insurance terms were staff shortages, petrol rationing and Excess Profits Tax!. It was agreed by the members of the Corporation of Brokers that they would not solicit business from one another so it was not easy for Mr. Packett to expand his business during this period. Constantly-changing and largely inexperienced clerical staff made it quite difficult even to service the existing connection satisfactorily. Two pillars of strength at the time, however, were the long-serving Kenneth Fox and the unrelated Miss Irene Fox who joined Mr. Packett as cashier in 1931 and served faithfully until her marriage in 1964.

The Packetts served a year as Deputy Lord Mayor and Lady Mayoress of Bradford (1940-41) although the purely social engagements were severely restricted. In the same year, their elder son, Charles Neville joined the firm as a junior and gained valuable practical experience before volunteering for the army in 1941.

1942 was a milestone in the history of the firm. In March, it became a private limited company, Sydney Packett & Sons Ltd., with Mr. Packett as Governing Director, the other directors being Charles Neville and Kenneth Fox. The founder's younger son, Sydney Duncan , like his brother, served in the family firm for a short period before volunteering for the armed forces, in his case the RAF. Both sons returned to the family business after the war and Duncan became a director.

The Post-War Years

With demobilised servicemen available for recruitment as extra staff and the acquisition of additional accommodation in Lloyds Bank Chambers, the business was able to expand rapidly in the 1950s. In Festival of Britain year (1951) a contract was first obtained from a statutory body, the British Wool Marketing Board, contracts followed by the National Pig Progeny Testing Board and the Potato Marketing Board. Today the firm has the privilege of accounts with two hundred authorities and Training and Enterprise Councils.

During the early 50s the firm decided it needed its own full-time fire surveyor and so, in 1954, a separate Fire Department and also an Accident Department were established.

The 60s - At Home and Overseas

The 50s having been a decade of expansion fairly locally, the firm now planned to move abroad.

In 1962, Mr. Neville Packett made the first of his many long-distance prospecting trips, this one to the far east. Later in the year, the Land and Marine Risk Commodity Insurance business of the Australian Wheat Board was obtained.

This huge account was secured after lengthy negotiations and against keen competition. In the following year. Mr. Neville visited Australia to service the Wheat Board connection. On the same extensive journey he managed to win business from the Australian Egg Board. To mark his travels to and interest in the Pacific, he received the Order of the Pacific from the Pacific Area Travel Association.

In 1964, the purchase of Frederick C. Wolfe & Son Ltd. meant the opening of a London office.

Finally in 1964 when the first of the Industrial Training Boards was set up, the firm was entrusted with the

Board's insurance arrangements. Subsequently they acted for most of the other ITBs.

The 70s - Further Expansion

On March 1st 1970, the firm celebrated its Golden Jubilee with a party. Business continued to flourish at home and abroad. In 1973, Mr. Duncan's elder son, Charles, the founder's first grandson, joined the firm, starting, like all the other members of the family, as just a junior clerk.

In the New Year's Honours List the following year, Mr. Neville was made an MBE.

When, in March 1977, Mr. Sydney Packett celebrated his 90th birthday, the staff gave a dinner for him at the Bradford Club. Later in the year, his second grandson, Andrew, joined the firm.

The Future

Sydney Packett & Sons celebrated sixty years of insurance business on March 1st 1980 with the founder attaining age 93 . He remained active until his death on 11th December 1980.

In order to keep pace with rapidly changing legislation and an ever-changing financial services industry, Sydney Packett (Life & Pensions) Limited was formed in 1987. The company is regulated by the Personal Investment Authority and offers independent advice to all clients, whether they are public companies or individuals planning for their future.

During the company's 78 year history it has developed a strong reputation for the quality of its insurance advice. As its clients' business activities vary, continued close contact with them helps to develop a full understanding of their particular insurance needs and enables them to tailor a more efficient professional and comprehensive personal service unique to them.

Today, Sydney Packett & Sons bears little resemblance to the firm of the 1950 and 60s. The company is now one of the north's largest truly independent insurance brokers and is of a size where it is able to give specialist advice in all areas of insurance and investment work. They have a considerable depth of resources and have harnessed computer technology so that their specialist departments can cover the major divisions of commercial work.

In today's rapidly changing business climate, the integrity and financial strength of a company is critical to its success. A measure of such integrity is the company's association with, and membership of, the Insurance Brokers' Registration Council, the British Insurance & Investment Brokers' Association, the Personal Investment Authority and the Society of Pensions Consultants.

Above: Mr Neville Packett receiving the Royal Medal of Merit (Silver) from H. M. The King of Tonga. **Facing page, centre:** The 'house sign' of the company which was adopted in 1957. **Facing page, top left:** Sydney Packett as he was in the 1980s.

Outskirts

Main picture: The Market place in Shipley showing the clock tower from the car park in 1962. The clock tower is one feature which brightens up this otherwise fairly characterless development. In many ways the half-dozen 'classic' cars look out of place in the picture, contrasting sharply with the square, concrete lines of the surrounding buildings.

Bottom right: This an another of Bradford's five-way junctions where traffic had a 'free for all' before a roundabout was built around 1955. At around this time trolley buses replaced the motor buses which had themselves the 1907 tram route down Fair Road to the terminus in High Street. St. Enoch's Road enters from the left. Standeven's Post Office was a thriving business serving people in this area with all their postal and newspaper needs; advertising boards for the Telegraph and Argus and Yorkshire Sports publications can be seen on their wall. This picture dates from around 1961.

Bottom centre: When constructed Odsal Stadium was intended to become the 'Wembley of the North.' Bradford Northern moved to Odsal in 1934 from the very unsatisfactory ground at Birch Lane. This aerial views dates from

before the time the roads were widened on the busy route between Halifax and Bradford, but after the time Websters (the Halifax brewer) took over the prime stand advertising positions. Formerly the name of Hammonds graced the rooftops here, but their brewing activities ceased in this area in the early 1970s. On the right of this photograph we can see the broad flat roof of Wilson's Gents Outfitters - later to become Odsal Police Station opposite Odsal Top roundabout.

Bottom left: An interesting picture of Oak Lane from Victor Road which dates from 1946. Most streets were gas lit at this time and the tall gas lamp on the left of the street would not have been out of the ordinary. Smoke can be seen belching from Lister's Mill chimney, the business no doubt in full production. The row of shops down to Victor Terrace ends with an Off-Licence - Hebden's which sold Guinness and Tetleys, and Heinz and Spratts... and, no doubt, Tizer. Down at Victor Street we see Jackson's Off Licence which advertised Hey's Gold Cup Ale and White Rose No. 5 Ales. Other adverts from the day, for Brooke Bond Tea and Bev Coffee essence add to the sense of nostalgia created by the picture.

W.S..

W.S..

W.S..

Edmund Bell - a national company with Bradford roots

In 1855, at the age of 22, Edmund Bell founded his business in Bradford. Little is known of the early days of the business, but Mr Bell was born in Lancashire, the son of a Wesleyan minister. As a

The two sons, Henry and Clifford, took over the business which was chiefly in dress goods, bulk cashmeres, bulk crepons and navy serges. Henry was educated at Trinity College, Cambridge where

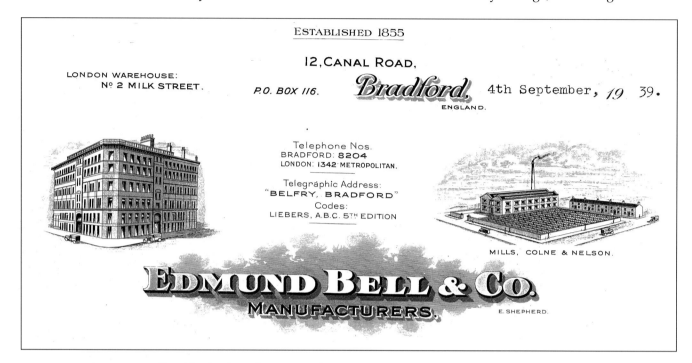

young man he came to Bradford where he married a widow whose husband had been in the textile business. He is reputed to have made so much money in the Franco-Prussian War (1870-75) that he built himself a new house in which the drawing room ceiling was coated with gold leaf. He also buried under the front doorstep newspapers, gold and silver currency, brandy and champagne.

In 1880, Mr. Bell took into the business a Mr Edwin Shepherd, then aged 14. In 1890 he died at the age of 57. The family were living at Rawdon and Mrs Bell ran things for a time, with the help of cashier, Mr W. Davy in financial matters.

he had gained his rowing blue and according to one of Bell's oldest customers, who had known Henry well as a youth, "Henry's father spent much time trying to regulate his son's youthful passions".

Henry became head of the firm but retired in 1903, two years after the death of his mother.

In November 1906 the business was taken over by a Mr Jenkinson and Edwin Shepherd. Henry died in 1915 and Clifford in 1926. In 1938, Mr. Keith Runton, then aged 30, joined as Export Manager. When, two years later, Mr. Shepherd died, Keith Runton raised capital from family and family contacts to buy the business and form it into a limited company. In 1947 the company moved premises from Canal Road to Chester Street as a result of purchasing W.H. Childe & Son. They remained there until 1997.

The company has always sought and deserved a reputation for long, loyal service from well-treated employees. An advertisement appeared in the Yorkshire Post in January 1960 for a typist. "This is a job for life for a fully competent and congenial

Top: A letterhead from the days when the company was based in Canal Road. Left: This order from April 1877 was for two types of fabric, one of 20 yards costing 27/6, about £1.37 today.

lady." When Mr J.W.W. Charlton retired after 53 years with the firm in 1970, the managing director,

Keith Runton, asked him in a letter, "Have you realised that you have served Bells for nearly half its lifetime? And....although you finish work today the results of your labours will never finish because they are now part of the goodwill and good name which you have helped to build?"

In January 1972, Mr Runton relinquished his office after 32 years, though he continued as Chairman and Executive Director. He was succeeded as managing director by Mr Neil Williams who served for 17 years before retiring in 1988 aged 61. Under his management the company made the key change from the garment trade and became a principal supplier of quality linings to the soft furnishing trade. He was succeeded by Keith Mitchell the present managing director.

Today Bells are the preferred supplier of furnishings to organisations who service the domestic and contract market in the UK and selected overseas markets. The company's main customers are the manufacturers of bespoke curtains. They have many long-standing wholesale and retail customers. Abroad, they supply the Scandinavian market and contracts in the Middle East. Their customers see them as a company committed to design, service, innovation, high standards of performance, people development and sustainable and profitable growth.

Above: This view, thought to date from the 1950s was taken from what is now the Boar's Well Nature Reserve, over Canal Road to the Bradford Power Station. Edmund Bell occupied premises on Canal Road until 1947, when the company moved to Chester Street. **Left:** *(From left to right) David K. Runton (present chairman), Keith W. Runton(MD from 1938 - 1971), E. Neil Williams (MD from 1972 - 1988) and Keith Mitchell (present MD).* **Below:** *The premises on Chester Street known as Belfry House. These premises were occupied between 1947 and 1997 when the company moved to its present site on the Euroway Estate.*

The wool success story

George Whitaker began his career with the railways because his mother wanted him to have a 'job with his coat on'. He failed the exams which would have led to a management position in the LMS and, older and much richer, said if he had passed them he might have ended his career as stationmaster at Frizinghall!

Next he joined the wool trade as an apprentice and was sent to the USA. At the first mill he visited he secured an order for 250,000lbs of wool tops. After 10 years he formed a partnership with his employer, Fred Towler before he formed his own company in April 1901. As it succeeded, it traded in wool of all origins, greasy, scoured and tops, and sold to the woollen and worsted mills in the UK, Canada and USA. In 1925, the company became incorporated under the title it still holds.

The offices of the company were at Swan Arcade in Market Street, Bradford, and it remained there until the move to Manorside Buildings in Manor Row in 1960. Manorside had been bought by the family as an investment in 1956 and used only as warehousing. Wool was stored, sorted and graded there. Part of the building was now converted to offices.

George Whitaker died in 1958 at the age of 82. From a very humble start, he achieved much for his family through determination and integrity. He had occupied every major office within the industry except that of President of the Chamber of Commerce. He had always treated his staff well and staff loyalty has been the strength of the company, some members staying for over 40 years.

George and Mary Whitaker had five sons and George had always used to maintain that his fortunes increased with the birth of each. Ralph joined the company in 1914 and stayed till his retirement in 1954. The third son, Basil, initially trained as a spinner with Roland Muff & Co. When he joined Whitaker's, he proved to be a clever financier and virtually ran the company from 1954 till his death in 1963.

1951 was the firm's Jubilee year. By this time the company had become the biggest wool merchants in the city, with offices in New Zealand, the USA and canada.

In 1951, during the Korean War, under the direction of George Whitaker and his sons, Ralph and Basil, the firm had frozen large amounts of stock by judicious anticipation of a new demand for clothing. As a result, the company achieved a higher level of profit than usual. Profits accrued over many years had already given the company stability, but this exceptional year was probably the reason why

it was felt prudent to release some of the capital for outside investment. So it was that, in March 1954, the company went into voluntary liquidation and reformed on the same day.

In 1956 a third generation of Whitakers entered the firm in the shape of David. He had served as an officer in the West Yorkshire regiment during National Service, then read economics and law at Cambridge. His cousins, Brian and Michael arrived straight from school.

In 1961, G. Whitaker & Co. (Export) was formed to extend export interests in western Europe but it was later decided to export only in the name of the parent company.

In 1966, Whitakers bought Haworth Scouring Company and, four years later, entered into trading synthetic fibres, which was to lead to becoming a third partner with Joseph Ogden and Company and Walker Brothers. Whitaker Fibres

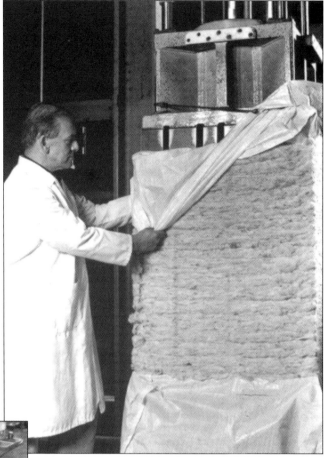

Simpson of Smith and Hayward, and currently Phillip Woodrow of Baker Tilly. Both gentlemen have been loyal friends to the family and its business concerns.

Above: The 500 tonne hydraulic wool press at the principal plant at Haworth. Left: The main scouring room at Lees Mill. Facing page, centre: George Whitaker, founder of the company which may not have existed had he not failed his exams! Facing page, bottom: A technical engineer adjusting the ultra-filtration plant at Lees Mill. Below: Oakwood, Court, Bradford.

was founded from this amalgamation in 1972 as a 100% owned subsidiary of the parent company.

Outside the Company, the family had other interests which embraced T. Collinson and Sons, Beech's Chocolates, Cuba Ltd., Manorside Ltd., Mitre estates and Chickens Cabins Ltd. which became the first UK franchisee of Kentucky Fried Chicken. The company's current premises are in Oakwood Court in City Road.

In all their business ventures, the family acknowledges a heavy debt to its financial advisors, first Herbert

Woods - the Genesis of good photography

From a 10 feet by 5 feet colour print for an exhibition to a multi-media presentation for a conference, from the developing and printing of one hundred rolls of colour film developing and printing to a web page for the Internet, Woods can deliver. For almost 70 years it has been involved in all aspects of visual communications.

From its small beginnings in Heaton in 1922 it has never stood still. Its founder, Charles Harold Wood, had been interested in motor cycles since his childhood when he dashed about the Bradford streets on a wooden scooter chalked with the name "Scott."

work for which it was most widely recognised. Another of his achievements was the developing of special goggles for training pilots to simulate night flying conditions. These goggles were used by the Dambuster pilots and earned Mr. Wood his MBE. After the war the business flourished, partly owing

In 1924 he was taken on by the Scott company, a Bradford based motorcycle manufacturer, as a works trials rider and combined this with his hobby, photography, eventually producing such films as 'Six of the Best' and 'The Roughriders'. Of his two interests, photography came to have the greater pull. He set up in a converted house in Manningham Lane, equipped with plate cameras and flash powder.

Aerial photography became one of his specialities and soon it was the aspect of his company's

to the fashion among mill owners to have an aerial picture taken of their premises for display on the wall.

Above: A Jowett Bradford van dating from around 1950. Below left: This leaflet was produced just after the war to offer mill owners and businesses aerial photographs of their premises. Below: Testing out a mobile camera in the late 1970s. David Wood is in the centre and the motorcyclist is Nick Jeffries, son of Saltaire Motorcycle dealer, Alan Jeffries.

AERIAL PHOTOGRAPHY

C.H.WOOD, 78, EMM LANE, BRADFORD

However, the company was conducting wide-ranging commercial and industrial work. Mr. C.H. Wood retired in 1970, the same year in which the firm moved into new, purpose-built premises in Leeds Road. The studio there was large enough to hold a fleet of cars if necessary and several different scenes could be shot there simultaneously. Ciné filming was becoming an important aspect of the work but colour and monochrome stills were taken there. With a studio ceiling 20 feet high, there was great flexibility in the use of lighting and angled shots. Introduced with the new building was the firm's ability to do their own colour printing on a new, computer-like machine. The day to day running of the photographic side of the business was looked after by director and son of the founder, Malcolm Wood. His brother, another director, David specialised in ciné film work. The two brothers are now the company's joint managing directors.

In 1984, Sir Keith Joseph officially launched the C.H. Wood Group 50th Anniversary celebrations by opening a new £75,000 extended studio. Sir Keith shot the first photograph, triggering off the studio's computer-controlled flash facilities. By now, the firm's high standard of work had attracted major international companies such as Shell, Rowntree-Mackintosh and Marks & Spencer.

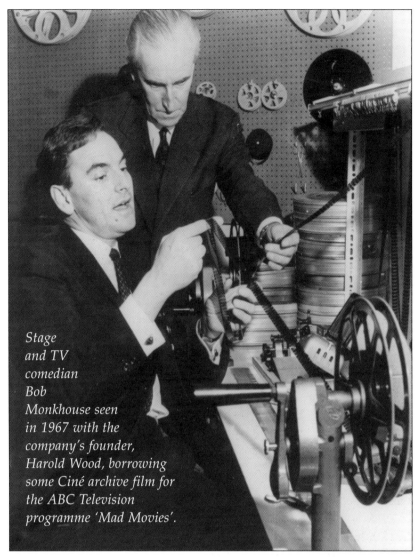

Stage and TV comedian Bob Monkhouse seen in 1967 with the company's founder, Harold Wood, borrowing some Ciné archive film for the ABC Television programme 'Mad Movies'.

During the last few years image technology has advanced dramatically.

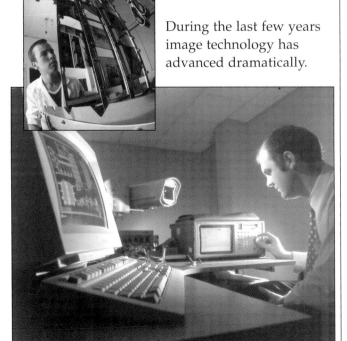

Now it is possible to produce giant colour pictures without ever using a photographic emulsion or chemical. Woods have therefore invested heavily in new digital technology. Photographs can now be taken by a digital camera, the images transferred to a computer for text and logos to be added before printing by a variety of devices. Unlimited graphic effects can be created. Any number of photographs can be combined together, colours changed, backgrounds altered and blemishes retouched.

Woods recognises that Bradford has become a centre for the computer and information technology industry and knows that it can offer Bradford businesses the most up-to-date and comprehensive visual communications services in the area.

The basic philosophy of Woods and its sister-company, Genesis, is one of quality and customer care. They don't just maintain standards, they set them.

Left, large picture: The new image technology in action. Left, smaller picture: Negatives in the firm's processing department.

Bird's eye view

Above: An aerial photograph of Queensbury, dominated by the impressive complex which is Black Dyke Mills which dates from 1835. John Foster and Sons are not the very large manufacturer of textiles that they once were, and the family home at Littlemoor has been demolished. It was situated by the tree-fringed fields at the top of the picture. The village is about 1130 ft above sea level at High Street, and over 1200 ft at the reservoir at Mountain. This makes it the highest inhabited part of Bradford. Soil Hill is 1300 ft above sea level and Oxenhope Moor is 1479 ft, but have no habitations.

The picture dates from the early 1950s when the houses were built on Brighouse Road at Hillcrest. At this time the local authority was the Queensbury and Shelf Urban District Council. Since 1974 Queensbury has been in the Bradford administrative area. Shelf is attached to the Calderdale authority. Holy Trinity Church at West End on the main road to Halifax was built in 1843 and had a tower added in 1906. It can be seen in the bottom-right corner of the picture, beside the A647 road to Halifax. The Hillcrest Estate can be seen at the top of the photograph on the right, at the side of the A644 to Brighouse.

Left: Clayton Heights from the air with Back Lane running across the centre of the picture from left to right. Highgate Road, running between Queensbury and the city centre, is on the left of the picture running at 45 degrees to the top of the photograph. The modern housing development in the middle of the scene is the Uplands Estate which was commenced in the 1950s by R.J. Patchett (Builders). The long established firm had built many houses in the district and their Ryfields Works can be seen at the top of this picture. On the left of the photograph we see the Asa Briggs Recreation Ground. In the foreground the group of modern houses laid out in three different cul de sacs off Back Lane was built by a different builder who, after a holiday in Ireland, named one of them McMahon Drive.

Above: This photograph dates from around the early 1960s, a time when housing developments started to take place on the open land to the west of Moore Avenue. The 1960s saw a determination throughout the whole of Britain to upgrade the Country's housing stock and reduce the waiting lists which had been growing since the end of the war. It took a tremendous effort to make an impact on the problem and reduce the number of insanitary dwellings. Moore Avenue was a new road from the Town Planning Scheme of 1928, built about 80 ft. wide and using unemployed labour on a 'week and week about' basis, i.e one week in two. Some of the men originated from the North East. The 'triangle' at Mount Road was the site of an early Wibsey reservoir. The road leading from the bottom (middle) of the photograph to the centre is Oakdale Avenue. It joins St. Enoch's Road which takes traffic into the centre of Bradford, off to the right. By 1945 trams were changing to Motor Buses and then to Trolley Buses in 1955, some going down Fair Road to the High Street terminus and some down Wibsey Park Avenue to the new Council housing estate at Buttershaw - built on Seed Farm. The roundabout in the five road junction would date from this time and Buttershaw is at the west corner of the picture. Wibsey Park Lane is unusual in that it forms part of the original water supply to Low Moor Iron Works which drew from the whole of the former Common - Wibsey Slack - upon which Buttershaw is built - and this was protected in the enclosure award of 1880.

Above: An aerial view of Odsal and Marshfields, showing the well-known roundabout at Odsal Top just left of centre, at the bottom of the picture. Left of the roundabout, the large building which was Wilson's Gents Outfitters headquarters, later to be the Police local headquarters, can be seen. The camera is pointed in the direction of the city centre, with Manchester Road running down the centre of the view towards Bradford. On the right of Manchester Road there is the clear, wide area of land which was known as Turncliffe, and used as a tip by the City Engineers Department. Later this area was to become the site of the Richard Dunne Sports Centre. This picture was taken before 1972 when Manchester Road was widened. The roundabout of the 1950s was replaced by a two-level interchange in that scheme.

Wibsey High Street and Holroyd Hill are on the edge of an escarpment with Carr Bottom Road 100yds away at the foot. Wibsey Bank is the steep road down to Bankfoot where the tram depot was built. The last tram, number 104, ran on route 15 and later found use as a score box. It was rescued by enthusiasts and restored. It is now an exhibit at the Industrial Museum. The tram depot has been demolished and replaced by a supermarket, but St. Matthew's Church has stood the test of time. Mayo Avenue can be seen with the open-space that would eventually have Morrisons Supermarket built upon it. The story of the rise of the Morrisons empire could fill a weighty volume in its own right.

An egg and bacon retailing business was founded in 1899 by William Morrison who operated it from Rawson Market. The business grew here up until it was bombed out in the Second World War. When the market was rebuilt in June 1958 Morrisons ran three specialist stores and a double shop unit in James Street. The James Street store was a significant milestone in the development of the firm as it was the first store in Bradford to offer self-service and to offer individually priced products. The firm introduced its first supermarket in the Girlington area in 1961. Truly massive growth followed which saw Morrisons dominate the grocery trade.

Below: Huddersfield Road, Low Moor - the A641 cuts across this picture diagonally, the northerly dual carriageway section being constructed in 1931 with the tram track down the central reservation. Curiously the Automobile Association objected to the dual carriageway proposal, saying that their members would not wish to be directed as to which portion of the road they could use! Several sett-paved crossings of the sleepered track were provided. The Wyke tram route ran through Low Moor and was operated using steam trams by the Bradford and Shelf Tramway Company from 1884 until the lease was recovered by the Council in 1900 (they actually owned the track); the route was then electrified and extended to Bailiff Bridge where it met the Halifax Corporation Tram system end-on. Low Moor Ironworks track can be seen bottom right, next to the dam which is now filled in. The 13ft high gateposts from this spot can be seen at the Industrial Museum, though they are now slightly reduced in height. The majority of the original Low Moor village has been pulled down and replaced by council development to the south-east of Huddersfield Road and north-east of Common Road. The Low Moor Picture Palace was opened in 1914, closed in 1957 and run as Pelican Bingo Club from 1964. The property is still standing at the time of writing. The old school has been rejuvenated and is now known as Hill Top First School. Netherlands Special School has been built on the large open area at the junction of Netherlands Avenue and Huddersfield Road which clearly shows the right-angled crossing of public footpaths. Low Moor Working Men's Club was opposite. The picture dates from around 1960.

Above: In this photograph Manchester Road can be seen following its sinuous course from the city centre towards Odsal. It replaced the even more sinuous, and narrower, Bowling Old Lane when the Turnpike Trust took the route over around 200 years ago. By 1972 it had been decided that widening was necessary in order to keep up with the demands of modern traffic and the road took on a new appearance, 100 feet wide with three carriageways. An underpass was incorporated at Odsal for good measure. In this view we can see that much of the preparatory demolition has taken place and road construction is about to begin. The site for the future City Technology College on Ripley Street is covered by fairly recent flat developments which replaced back-to-back dwellings.

The railway to City Road Goods Yard and Thornton had a station at Manchester Road and ran in a tunnel underneath St. Luke's Hospital - the former Union Work House. All Saint's Church was far too large for its situation, being built originally (by the Bradford Church Building Society) with an eye to it becoming Bradford's Cathedral, but this was not to be. The terraced housing of Marshfields and East Bowling have undergone renovation and remains. New Cross Street from Manchester Road to Bowling Old Lane has become Parkside Road which was cut off at Manchester Road. Bowling Old Lane is pedestrianised for much of its length and is more difficult to trace on the ground.

Right: This is a view of Fairweather Green Mills, occupied by the Greenside Woolcombing Company as they were known in 1966. The valley of the Bradford Beck is reasonably defined, cutting off the south-east corner of the picture and passing Sam's Mill which still supplies cattle food. Demolition has taken place at the mills fronting Cemetery Road due to the contraction of the wool trade. Housing developments cover the land to the south east of Sam's Mill and south west of Cemetery Road. The allotments to the south east of Thornton Old Road have also given way to housing. Crossley Hall First School occupies the building in the north west corner of the picture.

Below: This aerial photograph of Chellow Dean gives an excellent impression of the housing development created on the old Denby Farm by Heaton Estates between the mid 1950s and the mid 1960s. On the right of the picture we can just see the edge of Chellow Dean Lower Reservoir. Chellow Dean Reservoirs were amongst the earliest built for Bradford's water supply and received most of their water from Many Wells Springs near Cullingworth. They are now disused and form a park for the benefit of the general public.

The photograph is thought to date from the mid 1960s. Nearby Allerton village contained many textile mills, such as Smith (Allerton) Ltd., and another large industrial site making the cleaning liquid '1001' (advertised with the slogan: 'the big, big, cleaner, for less than half a crown' when I was a lad) opposite Ladyhill Park. Allerton Road can be seen 'cutting' the corner off the top left hand side of this photograph, near the terraced houses which remain to this day. On the right hand side of the picture there is a very distinct boundary between the built-up area and the fields leading to the reservoir. This is the line of the old Allerton Village by-pass, a road which has been abandoned.

Below and inset: This aerial photograph features the University and looks east towards the City centre. Here we see the new Institute of Technology building under construction in 1963, fronting Richmond Road. This route had originally been planned to be widened to become the City Ring Road at a lower level. The Institute became a university in 1966 with Harold Wilson as Chancellor. The houses to the right and below the University have been cleared since this picture was taken, to make way for student halls of residence, baths and further teaching facilities. The site being worked on here includes part of the area formerly occupied by Carlton Street School, the burnt-out shell of which was demolished shortly before this picture was taken.

The College of Art building is now the university library. Much of the mill property in the bottom left off the picture has now been cleared and the site redeveloped.

Construction of Bradford University's main building is well underway in this scene from the early 1960s. Fronting Richmond Road, off Great Horton Road the massive undertaking is almost complete in this picture, the work being carried out by contractors Higgs and Hill. The modern concrete-clad design contrasts starkly with the other buildings, mainly of Victorian origin, shown in the photograph. The University can trace its roots back to the formation of the Mechanic's Institute in 1832. Fifty years later, in 1882 establishment became Bradford Technical College, and later still, in 1957, the Institute of Technology. Harold Wilson was appointed Chancellor when University Status was achieved in 1966.

Above: This aerial view dates from 1966 and features the distinctive twin arches of the Exchange Railway Station roof. The span of the giant arches was almost the size of London's Kings Cross, a tremendous feat of engineering in 1880, the date the station was constructed. This was not enough to save the building when ideas were put forward for the redevelopment of this area, and it was demolished in 1976, just short of its centenary. The area is now the location of Bradford's Law Courts. The goods yard (seen here to the above and right of the station) was later to become the site of the Transport Interchange. A newly-constructed multi-storey car park can be seen to the right of this area. The vacant plot beside it was to become the home of the Norfolk Gardens Hotel. At the bottom of this scene the roof-top car park of C & A is visible, and, to the left of that the sunken walkway beneath Eastbrook Well/Petergate roundabout is shown, complete with newspaper kiosk in the centre of this unique location.

Above: An interesting aerial photograph of the City centre which shows the area before the wholesale redevelopment of the area began. Some demolition work can be seen in the Broadway area, and the fire which was later to destroy the property north of Forster Square had not yet occurred. Bradford's civic buildings can still be seen in the photograph, along with the Alhambra and the Wool Exchange. The property looks dark after years of exposure to the smoke from hundreds of domestic and industrial chimneys. One modern rooftop can be seen just to the left of the centre of the picture; it belongs to the Ritz Cinema and contrasts sharply with the narrow victorian rooftops of the other buildings in the vicinity. On the bottom right of the picture Forster Square can be seen, complete with covered bus and tram stands where passengers would board for the routes to the suburbs. At the time this picture was taken trams and trolley buses still served the public's travelling needs.

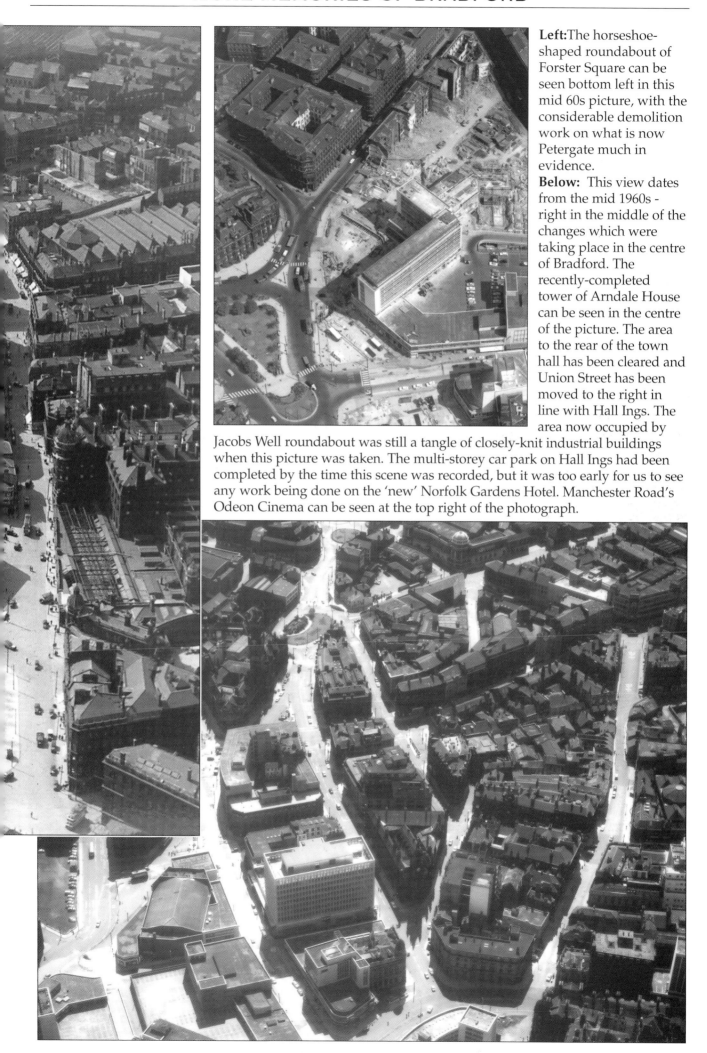

Left: The horseshoe-shaped roundabout of Forster Square can be seen bottom left in this mid 60s picture, with the considerable demolition work on what is now Petergate much in evidence.

Below: This view dates from the mid 1960s - right in the middle of the changes which were taking place in the centre of Bradford. The recently-completed tower of Arndale House can be seen in the centre of the picture. The area to the rear of the town hall has been cleared and Union Street has been moved to the right in line with Hall Ings. The area now occupied by Jacobs Well roundabout was still a tangle of closely-knit industrial buildings when this picture was taken. The multi-storey car park on Hall Ings had been completed by the time this scene was recorded, but it was too early for us to see any work being done on the 'new' Norfolk Gardens Hotel. Manchester Road's Odeon Cinema can be seen at the top right of the photograph.

A view of Bradford taken from just a few hundred feet above the Town Hall clock tower - well before the many changes which were to affect the town took place. Many familiar landmarks are shown, including the massive block at the bottom right of the scene is Britannia House which was once the home of O.S Wain's, better known as Ossie Wain's by most people. Just right of centre Brown Muffs large store is in view, adjacent to the Wool Exchange. A short walk in the direction of the right of the picture from this spot leads us to the Swan Arcade. On the left of the picture the dark, smoke stained buildings of the Town Hall can be seen with Bridge Street and Sunbridge Road running away from them to the top left of the photograph. On the extreme right we can make out the roof top of the Ritz cinema with nearby Broadway.

Above: A wealth of information is contained within this aerial photograph of the City. A little detective work reveals that the picture was taken in or around 1952; trams on the Queensbury route had been withdrawn from service in 1949 enabling an enhanced roundabout to be constructed in Victoria Square. This has now disappeared under Prince's Way, the central ring road, named after the Prince's Theatre which had been entered by the long passage from Little Horton Lane, this route is seen here going diagonally from the bottom left of the picture running upwards towards the right, in the direction of Wibsey. The Odeon Cinema of 1937 was demolished in 1970 to augment the site for the new Magistrates Courts and the Police Headquarters. At the bottom of the photograph, about a third of the way along from the left, we can see the broad roof of the New Victoria Cinema, later to become the Gaumont and now, at the time of writing, the Odeon 1 & 2. The original Wurlitzer theatre organ which once provided so much enjoyment here is now preserved at Howden le Wear in County Durham. The impact of the railway can be seen at the top left of the picture, with tracks veering off in a smooth curve to the left to Leeds, and contin-

uing in a straight line to Bowling Tunnel, Low Moor and Halifax towards the centre of the picture. The top right of the photograph shows the site of the City Technology College, though in this picture the Ripley Street area is still covered with orderly rows of terraced houses. Manchester Road can be seen snaking its way from the city centre towards the top right of the picture and the Hammonds Fountain Brewery building can be made out beside it near the top of the scene. The building was later demolished and part of the site now lies under the wider Manchester Road and the rest of it is part of the North British Housing Association site.

The open spaces on Bolling Road are now built upon. The area is an industrial estate which also covers the site of the demolished model village of Ripleyville.

Towards the bottom-left of the picture Town Hall Square and the semi-underground 'Crystal Palace' conveniences have gone, replaced by the Tyrrls and its fountain. The area of warehouses to the north of Croft Street between Nelson Street and Manchester Road was to experience the 'Great Fire of Nelson Street' in 1965, one of Bradford's most disastrous fires in recent living memory.

Below: The whole of the central area can be seen in this dramatic aerial view. There is a distinct contrast between the old and the new buildings, and the landscape has taken on a modern appearance with the sweeping curves of the modern inner ring road. The head office of the National and Provincial Building Society is in the final stages of construction. Meanwhile, the foundations for the Magistrates Courts and new Police Headquarters are being laid. Soon after this picture was taken the Exchange Railway Station would disappear altogether, and the Norfolk Gardens Hotel would be added to the scene beside the multi-storey car park. On the centre-left of the photograph the twin domes of the Alhambra Theatre can be seen, looking out with an unrestricted view in the direction of City Hall and the construction work which was to change the appearance of Bradford forever.

In this photograph the Magistrates Courts, opened by Her Majesty the Queen in November 1974, can be seen nearing completion. The multi-storey car park on Hall Ings has opened, as has a petrol station/car showroom beneath it. At the time of writing this property has been converted into a sports-outfitters. At the top left of the picture the distinctive curved frontage of the National Telephone Company is visible. This was later demolished to make way for Metrochange House; PTE offices, part of the Transport Interchange to be built on the Bridge Street Goods Yard site undergoing final demolition. The very large building just to the right of the centre of the picture is Wardley House. It opened in 1965 and commemorates the name of the City Engineer and Surveyor. Here the ice skating rink, Craywood Club (later, Mecca Bingo) and car park, shops and offices were located. It was a struggle to find the money to fully utilise the huge building until the birth of the National Museum of Photography Film and Television. In front of this massive building keen eyes may just be able to make out a trolley bus on Little Horton Lane. The era of the trolley bus ended in July 1971. The Horton Lane Congregational Sunday School building survives to the time of writing, as Glyde House, but the former influential Chapel has not been so lucky. The modern building behind Wardley House is the Central Library - opened in April 1967.

The Alhambra block has survived, the Alhambra itself being the subject of tremendous refurbishment and extension. Nearby Morley Street Picture House is no more, and the surgical goods shop went the same way, but the Queens Hall remains.

The Alexandra Hotel is seen on the left of the picture, beside Great Horton Road, it was demolished after a period of service as a student hostel. The Empire Cinema to its rear was pulled down some years before.

Prince's Way takes in the former New Victoria Street (which used to be known as Brewery Street) and Victoria Square. The site for the new Police Headquarters occupies part of the Whitakers Brewery area and the New Inn, demolished in 1964. The popular Inn had a plaque on the floor recording that it was at the very centre of Bradford. The top left of the picture shows a modern, square, white building which dates from 1970. It is the Provincial Building Society, extended in 1975 and destined to become the Abbey National.

Above: Taken about 1968, this photograph shows Wakefield Road improvement nearing completion. The railway from the south-west to the north-east is the line from Exchange Station to Leeds. All the property between Wakefield Road and Bowling Back Lane was subsequently demolished, but at the time the greatest loss was the Old Seven Stars public house.

The Prospect Hall was built in 1912 as it still tells passers-by. The octagonal chapel, as dictated by John Wesley, remains but it is now a Sikh Temple. The place of worship has been known as The Guru Nanak Temple since 1970. Usher Street School buildings remain in place, though their days as teaching facilities are long gone.

Facing page, smaller picture: We all have memories of fairs and fairgrounds from our childhood. The origin of fairs is linked with markets and the trade in horses, cattle, pots, pans and other goods. Regular *Fair Days* would be held in a town and these would attract side-shows and people selling food and drink to the crowds of buyers and sellers attending the event. Though there are still examples of similar combined markets and fairs in existence, but over the years travelling fairs are virtually always entertainment-related. Though not certain, we feel that this aerial picture features the fair at Peel Park. Memories of visiting fairs as a child are of the excitement brought on by the loud music, the sea of colours which characterised the swirling rides being watched over by the menacing, heavily-tattooed teenagers. We loved it of course, but our parents were often sick with worry until we returned home, penniless, but always with the obligatory goldfish or teddy-bear.

Below: In 1971 the construction of the M606 South Radial Motorway commenced to connect Bradford to the Motorway network via the M62. It was to have gone northwards to connect to a North Radial at Bridge Street, to go directly to Shipley and the Aire Valley, but this never happened. The overbridges carrying the roundabout never had a vehicle under them during 25 years until a new eastbound to south link was opened. The junction is called Staygate Interchange - being the local pronunciation of 'Staithgate.' Staithgate Lane used to meet Rooley Lane about the centre of the roundabout and was an old tram route from Low Moor pits, bringing coal to a staith there. Indeed, many stone sleeper blocks which carried the cast iron fish-bellied rails of the tramway were excavated on the length which was diverted around the primary electricity sub-station. Some of these shallow coal-workings gave the contractors considerable problems during the early stages of the work.

Above: Dudley Hill - before the demolition men changed the character of the area forever, is seen in this photograph from the late 1960s. The scene is dominated by the bold and busy roadways carrying thousands of vehicles every hour; Wakefield Road cuts diagonally from the top-left to bottom-right, and the road from Odsal, the A6036 Rooley Lane crosses it in the centre of the scene changing to Sticker Lane on its way to Laisterdyke, past Dudley Hill Social Club.

At the bottom of the picture the roof of The Picture Palace can be seen. The popular entertainment venue alongside Tong Street started life in 1912 and closed in 1967. The lovely old building was a perfect example of its type. After serving as a bingo hall for some years it later became a carpet retailers. Readers may remember the shops (mainly on the east side of Wakefield Road) including John S Drivers, Gallons Ltd., the chemists, and at least two banks, including the York County Savings Bank. Mills around the the junction included Scotts, Mulcott Belting and Ackroyds. The widening work for Wakefield Road was in full swing by 1968 and, in spite of being on a high-spot, the underpass works flooded in that year. We now have a two-level interchange with roundabout and slip roads at original ground level on the ring road. The Ebenezer Methodist Chapel located on Rooley Lane has, thankfully survived all the upheaval in this area.

Below: The Thornbury Works of Crofts Engineers dominates this photograph from the mid 1950s. The company was engaged in the power transmission industry and were later taken over by a larger concern. The main body of the works towards the east of Thornbury Road has been demolished, leaving their subsidiary, Carter Gears, to occupy part of the works towards the north of Thornbury Road. A school occupies part of the other site. Leeds Road, seen cutting across the corner of the bottom right-hand side of the picture, was the Turnpike Trust's replacement for Leeds Old Road (B6381) across the formerly unenclosed Bradford Moor at the top of the picture. It had to ascend Church Bank, from Forster Square and another short hill above Barker end Mills past the old Hanson School to reach the moor. Leeds Road enjoyed a better gradient or the horses to tackle up to Thornbury. Thornbury Laundry was at the easterly edge of the picture.

Above: This is probably Lister's Mill Chimney and Heaton Reservoir seen from the north in an era when smokeless zones did not exist. It certainly makes them seem like a good idea! The impact of smoke-controlled areas (a feature of the late 1950s and 1960s) on the health of local people cannot be underestimated. The introduction of smoke control was not universally welcomed - even by the ordinary residents it was intended to benefit. People complained that the new smokeless fuel burned quicker and less efficiently that the ordinary coal they were used to, and grumbled that they would no longer be able to burn their household refuse as they had done for years. Gas and electric heating were considered far more expensive than the coal they replaced.

> "THE INTRODUCTION OF SMOKE-CONTROLLED AREAS WAS NOT UNIVERSALLY WELCOMED - EVEN BY THE RESIDENTS IT WAS MEANT TO BENEFIT"

Below: Manningham Lane runs diagonally across this photograph which was taken before the disastrous fire which destroyed the Rolarena in 1955. The establishment was built in 1908 in the roller-skating boom that gripped the country. The Mecca Ballrooom was built on the site in 1960 - later to be re-named the Maestro. Eldon Place and Hanover Square still exist, the former as houses converted into business premises, and the latter as restored houses. Just to the right of Manningham Lane Bottomley's chimney can be seen. It used to carry its name in vertically-placed white glazed lettering, but the structure has now gone. Valley Road Goods Yard can be seen clearly at the top right of the picture; all that remains of this once busy rail facility is just one pair of tracks leading to the new Forster Square Station, with the land once used as sidings, as well as the former Power Station, now finding a new role as a retail park. The lower part of the picture, in the centre, contains the Belle Vue area. It gave its name to the barracks whose heyday was in the two world wars. It is used at the time of writing, by the Territorials. The hotel continues to thrive but Belle View Grammar School has relocated to Thorn Lane, leaving the buildings to be occupied by Manningham Middle School. The City Football Club ground had its disastrous fire in 1985 and is now rebuilt, but the houses to the east are demolished. Midland Road, that great wide way to nowhere has never realised its object - to run from Cheapside over Queen's Road through to Otley Road, Shipley. A vision of 1885 that never materialised. The Power Station cooling towers, once the largest installation of wooden cooling towers in the country, have gone - together with the Power Station - a very early municipal station which produced power right into the 1960s.

Above: This picture gives an overall view of the Jowett works which ultimately became the International Harvester tractor works. On Bradford Road we can see an open quarry. Idle's most prolific output took the form of quarried stone. This quarry and the rest of the Blakehill Quarries to the north-east have now been filled and built upon. The open area here has houses and the Police sub-headquarters upon it. A roundabout on Bradford Road gives access to Morrisons Enterprise 5 shopping centre which occupies the whole of the former Jowett works area. Norman Avenue is that curious dual carriageway route where once drivers could travel both ways on each side of the carriageway.

Left: Five Lane Ends can be seen virtually in the centre of this picture. The five original 'lanes' had all undergone extensive widening under private powers obtained from the Council's far-sighted Water, Gas and Improvement Act of 1873. Five Lane Ends is a part of Idle which has retained its now anomalous name in spite of the fact that the Corporation built an interloper in the 1920s called Swain House Road which, coupled with King's Road, formed the backbones of its large new housing estate. Trolley buses ran on Idle Road via Highfield Road to Saltaire (route 40), or via Bradford Road to Greengates (route 42), and to Five Lane Ends only (route 43) and turned at the time of this picture, in the junction without the aid of the roundabout which came later, in the mid-1950s. A combined tramway shelter and public lavatory was situated between Highfield Road and Bradford Road but this has long since disappeared.

The most famous product of Idle -apart from the Working Men's Club- was the Jowett car, using an economical horizontally-opposed engine. Models such as the Javelin and Jupiter (sports) are lovingly preserved by enthusiasts along with the famous 'Bradford' van. Manufacturing problems were encountered and the company eventually found itself in the hands of International Harvester Co., better known in the agricultural machinery world. Complete closure was to follow and the site was demolished and replaced by Ken Morrison's Enterprise 5 Shopping Centre. The Lane Ends Hotel survives as a public house.

Below: Wrose, looking towards the east in a picture dating from 1953. Wrose Road cuts boldly up the picture, North West, then West. This road is unusual in that it spanned two local authority areas, Bradford and Shipley, retaining its name in both, but suffering from the fact that the authorities could not agree on property numbering. Residents, and those wishing to contact them, therefore found it essential to mention 'Bradford', or 'Shipley' after the address, and to use the postcode. The old boundary crosses Wrose Road about two-thirds of the way up the photograph. The old Wrose village is is beyond the trees on the bend in Wrose Road. The village tree still survives in the middle of Low Ash Road. The Wrose Bull Pub and the Roman Catholic Church are in the trees. In Bradford Kings Road can be seen not to be extended northwards until the early 1960s. In the north east corner Idle Moor can be seen with evidence of the quarries and stone mines for which it was well-known. On the left of the picture the residential areas of the Thornacre Estate can be seen with Low Ash nearer the foreground.

Above: By 1955 work was well underway with the building of Bradford Council's new housing estate at Thorpe Edge, Idle, and we see many blocks of flats already built, or in the course of their construction. The Haigh Beck, between Parkland Drive and Haigh Beck View is still a feature of the estate. Thorpe Garth - Albion Road in the northerly corner of the picture is the Greengate's trolley bus route which by-passed Idle Village further to the north. Bradford was like scores of other towns and cities in the years following the end of the second war. There was a tremendous amount of poor quality housing in the area,

"IN THE 1960s, HIGH RISE FLATS WERE SEEN AS THE ANSWER TO THE CITY'S HOUSING PROBLEMS"

characterised by damp walls, no inside bath or toilet, over-crowded and badly heated. High-rise flats were one of the solutions settled upon by many local authorities in the 1950s and '60s in the struggle to get their long waiting lists down and to rehouse local residents in modern accommodation. In recent years certain estates and housing developments have acquired a poor reputation for a number of reasons, but it is easy to overlook the scale of the problem which faced local authorities and their ratepayers before the new developments were constructed.

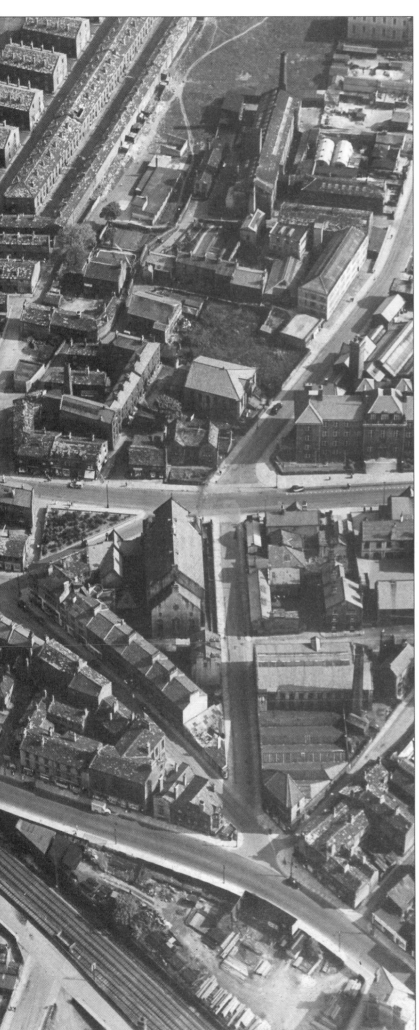

This picture dates from around 1950, before the Shipley central area was re-shaped by the Council. The Fire Station has closed, but has found a new use as retail shop premises. The Town Hall can be seen on the right, it dates from 1932, built on the site of the Manor House. The nearby Swimming Baths are also in view, they later found use as a restaurant and were replaced by a new facility in Alexandra Road. Kirkgate runs horizontally across the middle of the picture; the Baptist Church can be seen along side it. Rosse Street joins Kirkgate, it was named after Earl Rosse, a large landowner in Shipley. At the side of Commercial Street the roof of the Pavilion De Luxe Cinema (The Bug 'ole) can be seen. It closed in 1956 after providing local entertainment for 42 years. By 1970 the Fox Corner Improvement Scheme resulted in the demolition of the fine old building. At the time of writing the nearby Salvation Army Citadel and Labour Exchange building can still be seen in this locality, but all the property between the Pavilion and Glen Royal Cinema has been demolished. The old Market Place is now a section of dual carriageway. All the property south west of Kirkgate between Manor Lane and the back of property fronting Otley Road was demolished for the central area redevelopment of new Market place in the early 1950s.

This aerial view of the Market Place, Shipley is thought to have been captured around 1955.

Slightly above centre, the offices and showrooms of the North Eastern Gas Board (NEGAS) can be seen. Shipley was big enough to warrant its own branch of Woolworths, but at the time this picture was taken the Winhill Co-op had yet to be built at the Kirkgate end of the Market Place. Market Place Chapel still survives but the site between Kirkgate and Westgate is still to experience demolition prior to the erection of a market hall, shops and the clock tower. The Low Hall still stands, it is the Conservative Club as we write, as does the Post Office Sorting Office. The Post Office used to be located across the road, but later moved to premises situated where the fair is; in more recent times it became a franchise within the Asda store on Manor Lane. The railway station has lost much of its canopy, had its track re-organised and electrified, together with new track on the through-line linking Keighley and Leeds. On the right-hand side of Manor Lane there are buildings in view which would later be cleared to make way for Thomas Duggan House in 1980.

Right: Shipley from the air, with the gentle curve of Otley Road on the left of the picture, with adjoining Market Street on its right. The Arndale Centre is the square building almost exactly on the centre of the scene. At the top-right corner we can see Manor Lane and the houses beside it which were later to be cleared right through to Bradford Road and St. Paul's Road. At one time it was expected that the site would be occupied by Inland Revenue Offices, but this turned out not to be the case. Eventually ASDA developed the site and built a new public library and smaller retail shops as part of the project. The building of a new library resulted in the closure of the town's two other libraries.

At the bottom right of this photograph Kirkgate can just be seen below the 'E' shaped building, opposite Market Place which houses Woolworths.

Below: This is a view of Windhill, originally a separate Local Board, then part of Shipley UDC, now in Bradford. The original Leeds and Bradford Railway of 1846 crosses the lower half of the picture with the Colne extension to Keighley of 1847 just in view. In the battle for custom the Great Northern Railway built a line from Laisterdyke to Windhill in 1875, giving Windhill its own station on Leeds Road which closed in 1931 but is still standing today. The bridges on the bottom left hand side of the picture carry the railway over the Bradford Canal whose pump house still stands on Dock Lane. Butterfield's Tank Works from Charlestown had a factory at Low Well below the Gas Holder.

The Carnegie Library of 1906 at the junction of Carr Lane and Leeds Road (almost in the centre of the picture) is now closed but the church and school further up Leeds Road remain. The school next to the Great Northern Goods Yard is now a cat museum - 'Forever Feline' which succeeded the Sooty Museum. The Blue Bell pub at the bottom of Carr Lane and its neighbour The Shoulder of Mutton still survive at the time of writing. The Liberal Club is no longer 'Liberal' and is empty as we write. The picture is almost half a century old now, and during this time many houses have been cleared, such as those between Leeds Road and Hall Lane, and those South-West of the Carnegie Library, most replaced by council housing.

Above: Shipley's main shopping streets were Kirkgate and Westgate, together with Commercial Street, Briggate and part of Otley Road. In the process of creating the new Market Square, seen here almost complete, in the mid 1960s, all of the shops in Kirkgate and one third of the shops in Westgate were pulled down, along with two streets of houses. The result is pleasant, if somewhat bland, and the Market Square has been made traffic-free except for buses and some access. Some people want it making even more bland by the demolition of the clock tower!

The Arndale Centre is an early, but small example of Sam Chippendale's developments.

Manor Lane Chapel can be seen right in the centre of this photograph; the church remains to this day, though the Baptist Chapel is now a car park - worship now takes place in the former Sunday School. The junction of Commercial Street/Briggate with Otley Road at Fox corner was improved in 1974 and necessitated the demolition of the Fox and Hounds, two Banks and another swathe of shops.

The area north of the canal has, in the main, been demolished - notable exceptions being Jerome's and Mason's Mills. There is now a new road through this area, 'Salt's Mill Road' hurriedly changed from 'Old Mill Road' linking with Victoria Street, then through to Salt's Mill via a new bridge over the canal with a branch to the open area west of Jerome's Mill. This contains the new Inland Revenue facility at Jane Hills. The bridge carrying Victoria Street over the canal has been renewed and the street extended over the railway to Commercial Street.

Below: This aerial view of Gilstead was captured looking in a roughly southerly direction. Bingley Urban District Council developed a housing estate looking down the hill to Cornwall Road from the south west side of Gilstead Lane. The south east side, down Primrose Bank, and the north west side were constructed privately, augmented in recent years by Pendle Road and Rombalds Drive on the site of a quarry and a stoneworks. Stone is no longer quarried on this extensive escarpment to the west towards Micklethwaite. The Gilstead Filter Beds have undergone drastic reconstruction works by Yorkshire Water in recent years. They were among the earliest parts of Bradford Corporation Water Works, being situated on the Barden Aqueduct of 1854.

The old centre of Gilstead survives around the junction of Primrose Lane and Gilstead Lane. Several houses were swept away during the widening of Gilstead Lane on the recreation ground frontage before the last war. St. Wilfrid's Church ceased holding services here in the mid 1990s.

Above: This elevated photograph from the early 1950s is bound to bring back memories for anyone with an interest in the history of local aviation. This is the site of Leeds Bradford Airport, though at the time this picture was taken it was, of course, known as 'Yeadon Aerodrome.' It is interesting to see the large hangar buildings still in their wartime camouflage colours and the 1950s motor cars dotted around the main airport building which add atmosphere to the scene.

Left: Memories of Baildon are certain to be evoked by this interesting aerial photograph from 1963. Baildon is an ancient village originally on the route from Bingley to Otley. The centre of the village is Towngate, 'gate' being derived from the word gata being an old name for a street. Many of the street names reflect the old origins of Baildon e.g, Browngate, Westgate and Northgate. Moorgate was probably an actual gate onto the Common - Baildon Moor - of which Baildon Bank is a large detached part. In this picture we can see the footpath which zigzags up the very steep incline of Baildon Bank on the bottom left,

starting at Green Road. Another footpath can be seen crossing it, almost at right-angles from Green Road to Bank Crescent, a more gentle slope except for the steep bit at the top. It passes Lane End, that interesting jumble of houses which was later demolished in the orgy of slum clearance which affected towns and cities like Bradford in the years after this photograph was taken. Baildon had its town hall in Rushcroft Terrace, almost central to this scene. The U.D.C had disappeared in 1974 and the town hall serves as a care home for the elderly at the time of writing. In this photograph the Mechanics Institute had not yet been demolished, but the redevelopment which was to reshape the town centre had already begun. Newton Way, which was to give improved access via The Grove to Lucy Hall Drive, was yet to be constructed.

A dramatic aerial view of Bingley, dominated by four different transport features which converge within a hundred yards of each other in this photograph. The main Keighley Road dissects the picture from top to bottom, running into Bradford Road as it nears the top of the photograph. The gently curving River Aire is just in view on the right, and the 3-rise locks of the Leeds and Liverpool Canal and the sweeping curve of this popular, historic waterway are on the left. Since this photograph was taken the canal has been moved westwards (left, in this picture) to yield about 30 yards or so for the continuation Southwards of the Aire Valley Trunk Road. Whether this project is ever completed remains to be seen. Between the road and the canal we see the railway line and associated Goods Yard beside it. Towards the centre of the photograph the Midland Railway Station which dates from 1882, is clearly shown; the station remains, almost as it was built, to this day. It was the subject of some refurbishment when the line was electrified. The South goods yard is now a car park.

Bingley's slum clearance from fifty years ago produced the 'folly' conveniences which themselves disappeared to make way for Ferncliffe Road down to Dubb Bridge from the Top O'th Town and the Myrtle Walk Shopping Centre. Demolition in the 1950s and '60s removed the 'Seven Dials' junction of seven streets, along with many houses from the east. Demolition from Top O'th Town to the west of Main Street down to Myrtle Place produced a site for the Bingley Building Society which was later extended to give an 'ocean liner' and 'Hanging Gardens of Babylon' effect when it became the Bradford and Bingley Building Society.

Acknowledgments

The publishers would like to thank the following people for their help in making this book possible:

Brian & Dorothy burrows

Wood Visual communications

Walter Scott (photographers)

The staff at bradford central library

Reprints of photographs

All photographs with the initials 'ws' are copyright of Walter Scott (Bradford) Limited, who can supply reprints.

Reprints for most of the other pictures within this book are available. For further details please contact the publishers (address on page three of this book).